RESPONSIBLE ABANDON

RESPONSIBLE ABANDON

STRUCTURED PLAY AS GROUNDS FOR CREATIVITY AND INNOVATION

DEVIKA KUMAR

NEW DEGREE PRESS

COPYRIGHT © 2018 DEVIKA KUMAR

RESPONSIBLE ABANDON

Structured Play as Grounds for CREATIVITY and INNOVATION

ISBN   978-1-64137-145-2 *Paperback*

          978-1-64137-146-9 *Ebook*

To my family, who taught me to think adventurously, give generously, and, most importantly, dream fearlessly.

CONTENTS

A BRIEF REFLECTION ON MY EDUCATION

FIRST GRADE

I sit on my car seat and name the dancing raindrops on the windows as I watch their friendships develop. They slide down the car in frenzied spirals and collide to make bigger raindrops and then self-divide to clone themselves. I take out my sketchbook and draw what I see—how raindrop-Phillip and raindrop-Erica combined to make a super-raindrop, capable of defeating all the other drops in the land.

The allegro rain pounding on the roof of the car dwindles to a lento staccato as we get home and my mom unbuckles my car seat so I can run out to find my sisters. I smell sunlight burning pavement puddles into mist and floating up against a dim yellow sky, and I wonder if the trampoline is dry. As the clouds part, I grab my sisters' hands and we run and jump and slide around for hours and hours until my mom yells, "Come in now or the deer will give you ticks!" So I go in and drink chocolate milk and eat potato fries and dress up my baby sister in boys' clothes.

THIRD GRADE

I present my 3D model of a scene from the book *Flat Stanley*—a 2D book—so it's my first attempt to game the system. I answer questions, and everyone claps. I share goldfish with my best friend Carmen at lunch and then rush to the seesaw where I meet my other best friend Tej for our daily adventure.

Up, down, up, down—each down is worth it because I know I'll be up soon again. We play for 30 minutes and then go inside and trade the seesaw for cursive practice, playing with letters instead.

Criss-cross on the carpet next to frizzy Erica and glasses Phillip, I wiggle my toes impatiently waiting for dismissal. Mrs. Sharma assigns us our chores for the week—botany, my favorite—and reminds us to memorize our lines for our class play. Then, "You are dismissed!" Giddy, we bounce to our cubbies to get our things and race to the door. The faster I leave, the sooner I can play at home.

FIFTH GRADE

Math and science in the morning, where I glue two soda bottles together to make a terrarium and aquarium with real fish and real snails. I feed and observe animals grow in the artificial natural habitat I created. Then I learn about magnetism by seeing who could spell their name with magnets and iron filings.

In computers, I log on to the pink flamingo typing game and try to beat my high score because the highest scorer picks a surprise toy from the bin. Then I employ my fast fingers to write a story about Maria meeting Leppy the Leprechaun on St. Patty's Day and their adventures in the secret Irish "Narnia."

SEVENTH GRADE

Math is now basically English, and unsolvable algebraic expressions plague my very existence. But no homework during recess, so I go to the basketball court with Chris and the boys. We play Horse until Mr. Madani makes us come inside to find "x," but I want to tell him to find it himself.

Locked inside until tennis practice after school, we play "no bounce rule," which becomes a frantic free-for-all of rackets swinging and balls flying. Then I go home, finish homework, watch TV, and sleep.

NINTH GRADE

High School. We clap every time someone goes up to the board to do a "star" problem in our 10-student Honors Geometry class with Mr. Asch. We get 60s and 90s, but he grades our progress, so we get rewarded for trying. Mrs. Shepard asks me how my sister's theater performance went, and I ask Mr. Cara how his son is liking BU. I know all of my classmates by first name, so we're in it together.

In our thirty-minute lunch period, I sit by Mr. Asch to go over homework problems and talk about why Roger Federer is the greatest player of all time. He gives me some of Mama Gina's homemade zucchini bread before I go to my next class.

SENIOR YEAR

Welcome to College Counseling seminar, where we 18-year-olds plan the rest of our lives and pretend to know what we want even though we don't know what we want for lunch. "Make sure you have good extracurriculars!" And "SAT scores matter," and "don't write about parents or overcoming obstacles." But these admissions officers read millions of apps a day and don't even know me.

"Hush, hush," don't ask about ~college~ because it's ~sensitive~ so instead lie to your friends about where you applied. And it's okay to be lazy too because "senioritis" is widely accepted especially when you get into a college because school isn't about learning or challenging yourself but rather getting into college.

***

I am lucky to have had such a great experience with school until college, and I credit that mostly to the classes I took and the teachers I met at Princeton Day School. As a total nerd, I loved the individual attention I received in class. I loved becoming friends with my professors and asking them about their kids. I especially loved how I paid attention in nearly every class and actually, actively learned things.

But then, college happened.

COLLEGE

I sat in the back of my macroeconomics class, scrolling through Facebook while I saw nearly all the screens in front of me do the same. I didn't need to listen to the labor productivity slowdown because I saw it in front of me, so I plugged in a headphone and listened to music. After class, I bartered with friends so Liam would send me the first half of questions and Steph the second and in exchange I would send Liam the second and Steph the first.

Wasn't college supposed to be a place of intellectual discovery, collaborative brainstorming, and youthful vigor? Why am I bored? Why are my friends bored? **Why do we feel like we're living in the moments between chunks of frustration and faking our way through classes we don't care about?**

As an upperclassman who jumped hurdles to get permission to invent my own major (yes, I made it up, and yes, it is legit), I expected things to be different. I get to select each class I take, so I should love them all, right? People major in things they like because they can take classes about things that are supposed to be interesting. But plot twist, they're usually not.

A 2013 Gallup poll of 500,000 students in grades five through 12 found that nearly eight in 10 elementary students were "engaged" in school. By high school, that number dropped to four in 10. A later study found than less than a third of 11th graders felt engaged. When teens were asked to describe how they feel in school, half of the students chose the word "bored", followed by "tired" as a close second, with 42 percent. Sadly, even in college, 45 percent of recent dropouts listed boredom as a "major" or "minor" reason they left.[1]

Some of the reasons why boredom escalates are intuitive, such as the increased emphasis on standardized tests that accompanies growing up. When teachers are required to teach to a test, teachers and students both lack freedom, leading to overall disengagement in the classroom. Similarly, each year, school becomes less and less new, so repetition too begets boredom.[2]

The more interesting explanation is that we shift from creative and experiential learning to one that is more cerebral and regimented.

Trust me, I love debating philosophy and writing research papers, I really do; but, I also love chopping wood and making paper mache masks. I love solving math problems, but I also love catching butterflies and collecting leaves. There is undoubtedly merit to putting your head down and pushing through periods of boredom to develop work ethic and strengthen your weaknesses. But, in limiting learning to

---

1 Jason, Z. (2017). *Bored Out of Their Minds.* [online] Harvard Graduate School of Education. Available at: https://www.gse.harvard.edu/news/ed/17/01/bored-out-their-minds [Accessed 6 Nov. 2018].

2 Ibid.

slides on a computer, we're missing an opportunity to motivate students and maximize learning.

Interestingly, Jill Goldberg, Ed.M from Harvard, says some of the blame is on the parents. When she asks her students why they're in school, they tell her it is "because their parents work so this is where they need to be during the day." They say that school is to them what jobs are to their parents. So when we think about what motivates parents to work, most would likely say that they work to make money."[3]

OPTIONS

I am lucky my parents are spectacularly different. My dad grew up in India not very wealthy, but rich with dreams, and came to America with nothing more than $20 in his pocket and a desire to make something of himself. My mom, on the other hand, grew up with wealth that suddenly disappeared, forcing her to relocate to Queens where she lived alone at age 16. Together, they built a successful network marketing business, among other business assets, that has empowered them with financial freedom and an unparalleled lifestyle of adventure.

---

3   Ibid.

My parents don't have a job; they work for themselves. Ever since I was little, they have been able to drive me and my sisters to school, come to our tennis matches, and stay up late finishing our homework with us. Because they love the life their business has granted them, they taught us to think like investors, with an asset-based mindset. We've been going to business conferences several times a year, and truthfully, that's where I received the most practical and relevant education.

At these conferences, I see people who have nothing become something. I hear Somalian refugees who risked their lives in pursuit of the American dream tell their success story with humility and confidence. I see college dropouts, possessed with the dream of financial freedom, trade sweats for suits and become mentors for others. I observe bad students read a book a night, committed to improving their resilience and street-smarts. I learned the importance of concepts like The Law of Attraction, Self-Image, Written Goals, Attitude, and more. What I learned from the business has been more practical and important than anything I learned at school.

I realized that the most important learnings often happen beyond the 9–5 of school or work.

I always saw school like my parents saw their business: an opportunity to learn and grow while adding value to others. I would go from school, where I learn, to business conferences, where I learn again, receiving two educations at the same time. But my sisters and I are immensely privileged, and forever grateful, that our parents are passionate about their lives. We're the exception.

If students look at how most parents treat jobs they're not passionate about as models for how they should treat school, I understand why students end up bored.

I observed a pretty sad phenomenon this summer, when I commuted from a night job in New Jersey to a day job in New York.

The New Jersey Transit 2.5-hour commuter experience, from Princeton Junction to New York City, still haunts me. Show up five minutes before train leaves. Get the express or you're late to work. Run, run, run to the platform. Swarm the door when the train stops. Walk up and down, wiggle into a seat, pull out a phone or sleep. No talking, no smiling. Train stops, subway to work, work, subway back, and repeat.

Robots.

I don't doubt that these people work hard, and for good reason, too. We need to work to make money to survive. There is such a thing as delayed gratification, of course. But, there is also such a thing as living up to your potential as a human being. Sadly, people are too familiar with trudging their way through life sacrificing interest, joy, and pleasure for titles and prestige. I know that when the commuters were children, they enjoyed more and were much more enjoyable to be around.

So, what changes? When do we go from free-spirited ragamuffins to robotic commuters?

I think it happens when we stop having structured play. We used to have recess, which was time carved out for us to play freely. Then, we still had activities, like sports, with some kind of structured time. But eventually, people stopped structuring play for us, forcing us to fill that time ourselves.

We either fill it to maintain that element of play, fill it with school, or fill it with work.

The education system does little to help emphasize the power of play. Now, I don't at all suggest we emphasize arts over math and science. Trust me, I love few things more than I love my geometry proofs and phospholipid bilayers. Instead, **we need to create a culture in schools of design thinking,** hypothesizing, and experimenting, blurring the lines that separate disciplines and, in general, one that values learning for the sake of exploration over end-of-semester performance.

Even though school hasn't changed enough yet, ('m working on it!), I believe we can make an individual effort to choose to integrate play into our lives. In other words, while we may not have play time structured for us, we can see the world as our playground to learn as much as possible and stay creative like kids.

"Creativity is the residue of time wasted."

– ALBERT EINSTEIN

INTRODUCTION

———

Coffee. Foamy fumes waft through the air, wrapping a light fog around silhouettes crowding tables. Pastries warm behind the counter, tempting iced-coffee refills with sweetness. Artists pull their hair back with pencils behind their ears, balancing tattered books in one hand and lattes with the foam trees in the other. Intellectuals chitchat in the back booth debating politics, math, philosophy, and more. People don't schedule their interactions but just interact. Everyone has their own table with their own work, but the spontaneity of collaboration takes priority.

In the seventeenth century, London coffeehouses became extremely popular. In contrast to Taverns, which served as places to drink copious amounts of alcohol and gamble, coffeehouses were more conducive to conducting business.

For a single penny, men (still not women… yet) could gain admittance into a coffee shop and stay for as long as they liked with no obligation to purchase anything.[4]

Everyone flocked to the coffeehouses to debate, close deals, play board games, distribute pamphlets, and, on occasion, drink a cup of coffee. Polite conversation led to thoughtful debates about everything from politics to poetry, so much so that English coffeehouses became known as "penny universities," where people like Isaac Newton, Alexander Pope, and John Dryden did some of their most influential thinking.[5]

These "penny universities" became centers of commerce that often bred revolutionary innovation.

Some notable examples include:

- Jonathan's Coffee House in 1698, where men met to set commodity stock prices. Later became the London Stock Exchange.[6]

---

4   Green, Dr. 2017. "The Surprising History Of London's Fascinating (But Forgotten) Coffeehouses". *The Telegraph*. Accessed November 6 2018. https://www.telegraph.co.uk/travel/destinations/europe/united-kingdom/england/london/articles/London-cafes-the-surprising-history-of-Londons-lost-coffeehouses/.

5   "The Enlightenment Coffeehouses | Conversational Leadership". 2016. *Conversational Leadership*. Accessed November 7 2018. https://conversational-leadership.net/coffee-houses/.

6   Ibid.

- Lloyd's Coffee House on Lombard Street, run by Edward Lloyd, where merchants, underwriters of chip insurance, and shippers met to do business. Later became Lloyd's of London, one of England's longest-lasting insurance companies.[7]
- Salesrooms attached to several coffee shops held auctions that became early homes to Sotheby's and Christies.

These coffeehouses, designed specifically for leisure, were clearly contributing to society. Yet King Charles II tried to ban them because he thought people were wasting their time breeding fruitless ideas.[8]

He didn't realize that coffee shops were bastions of innovation, namely *because* they were designed for leisure. Without that allocated leisure time and space, invention perhaps may never have occurred like it did.

In his book *Wonderland: How Play Made the Modern World*, Steven Johnson cites example after example of "artifacts from the future," or things that are "dismissed as mindless

---

7 "Edward Lloyd And His Coffee House.". 2018. *Lloyd's Register*. Accessed November 7 2018. https://www.lr.org/en/who-we-are/ brief-history/edward-lloyd-coffee-house/.
8 "English Coffeehouses". 2018. *Historic UK. Accessed November 7 2018. https://www.historic-uk.com/CultureUK/ English-Coffeehouses-Penny-Universities/.*

amusement" in their time but turn out to have ripple effects for generations to come.[9]

The music box is my favorite example. An old music box used to play multiple songs depending on the code you put inside it. This mysterious code technology stayed a secret amongst musicians for the longest time, until one guy decided to take a closer look one free afternoon. He looked into the music box code and expanded upon it to develop punch cards. These punch cards became an invention – the Jacquard loom – that dramatically changed the textile industry. Some other guy years later looked into the loom in his free time and took those punch cards to create the first programmable computer.[10]

None of these people would have explored the mechanism behind these items without free time. They needed time to be creative.

PLAY AND CREATIVITY

IBM surveyed 1,500 CEOs across 60 nations and found that creativity is one of the most critical skills for the future.[11]

---

9 Johnson, Steven. 2016. *Wonderland.*
10 Ibid.
11 "IBM 2010 Global CEO Study: Creativity Selected As Most Crucial Factor For Future Success". 2018. *Www-03.Ibm.Com.* Accessed November 7 2018. https://www-03.ibm.com/press/us/en/pressrelease/31670.wss.

The most inspirational people—entrepreneurs, innovators, change-makers—possess an enviable ability to take chances, dream big, and create the things we need. Most would agree that in our quickly changing world, we need people who can adapt to new ideas, problem-solve, and take unprecedented risks. So yes, the modern world craves creative people, but I'm sure that's not surprising.

The question is, how do we get more creative?

Albert Einstein famously said, "**To stimulate creativity, one must develop the childlike inclination for play.**" Pablo Picasso also said, "**Every child is an artist. The problem is how to remain an artist once we grow up.**" AKA, let's not become boring adults.

Many studies have examined the relationship between play and creativity. A notable study conducted in 1967 by Brian Sutton-Smith, a leader in the field of play theory, showed that participants who were told to imagine various purposes for an object they had not seen came up with more ideas, on average, than those who were given the object first. Paul Howard-Jones and others corroborated Smith's findings in 2010 when they found that students who were given 10 minutes of free time to play with playdough before doing a task enforced more creative ideas than those who were not.[12]

Having time to play gives you the freedom to think, connect, and interact meaningfully and creatively.

Children have recess and play-dates specifically to support exploration. Now, without structured play, we no longer have the time allocated for thinking freely and exploring; as a result, our creativity becomes stifled.

When I asked my eccentric creative writing professor, Tom Quigley, how he became who he is today—a man who grades papers with Crayola markers, takes his students for walks in the woods, and forces them to play on the playground—he said "I knew I had to grow up. But did I have to grow up and be miserable? I didn't want to be miserable like all the adults I saw around me."

And there it is. **We don't have to become boring adults.** No offense to those of you who already are. We probably need y'all too—to become tax auditors and macroeconomics lecturers.

---

12 Christensen, Tanner, and Tanner Christensen. 2014. "Why Play Is Essential For Creativity". *Creative Something.* Accessed November 7 2018. https://creativesomething.net/post/84134598535/why-play-is-essential-for-creativity.

But playing like kids liberates us from the dreary seriousness and stress of adulthood, simply by freeing us to alter our perspective of reality. Kids *imagine* and *daydream* and use corners of the brain adults forget we have.

Somehow, somewhere, maybe through the education system, experiencing hardship, or realizing that we need money to survive, we become somewhat complacent with basic assumptions that ought to be questioned. Our leisure time tends to dwindle, so we play less, become less creative and more boring, learn less and memorize more, and connect less and network more.

Play is the antidote to a predictable adult life. Play is the way to preserve all those traits kids have so we can live freely and creatively.

HOW TO PLAY

Before writing this book, I felt stifled. Even though I go to one of the best schools in the country, somehow I felt unfulfilled—like I wasn't living or learning up to my potential. This book gave me permission to explore.

In my attempt to discover what to write about, I rekindled my dying passions for architecture and creative writing. I cold-called people who I found fascinating just to learn a little bit about their experiences. I reinvigorated my life with a purpose to grow my passion project, my most important project, even though it was ungraded. Most importantly, I became less risk-averse, more conscious of what I want, and more inclined to give life to out-of-the-box thinking.

All of those things helped me not only learn more and live happier but also get a job, for which I had little to no experience, as the first hire at a real estate tech startup this past summer. I applied on AngelList, and after my now good friend but then stranger, Tom, interviewed me, I received a business development research project. The task was to essentially reach out to house flippers in Charlotte, North Carolina, and try to get them to send me as many data tapes (property sheets) as possible.

"You have one week. Present the deliverable in an output that makes sense." Most people think "PowerPoint time!" I happen to think PowerPoints are extremely boring, especially if nobody is there to present them in person. So I made a website with sections like "Strategy," "Mistakes," and "Learnings." In this one week, while I managed to accidentally cost realtors $200 (whoops), I used my newly-developed cold-calling skills and confidence in my creativity to fool my bosses into hiring me. (Gotcha, Tom and Cyril!)

Play fundamentally changed my perspective of what I can accomplish. Play unlocked for me what two of my favorite people, Tom and David Kelley, coined as "Creative Confidence." David Kelley, the founder of Ideo and Stanford d. school, animates creative confidence when he recalls the following story of when he was in elementary school.

One fine school morning, David saw his friend, Brian, playing with some clay. Their teacher always left clay under the sink, so Brian decided to make the clay into a horse.

At one point, one of the girls that was sitting at his table, after seeing what he was doing, leaned over and said to him, "'that's terrible, that doesn't look anything like a horse!' And Brian's shoulders sank, and he wadded up the clay horse and he threw it back in the bin. I never saw Brian do a project like that ever again."[13]

People opt out of thinking of themselves as creative as they enter into adulthood. They have a clay horse incident like Brian's and dismiss themselves as "not creative" simply because they aren't "the creative type." But creative confidence is all about redeeming our natural state of creativity and growing

---

13 Kelley, David. 2018. "How To Build Your Creative Confidence". *Ted. Com.* Accessed November 7 2018. https://www.ted.com/talks/david_ kelley_how_to_build_your_creative_confidence?language=en.

our self-efficacy (i.e. the belief that we can attain what we set out to do.)[14]

And it's not just with creativity. Some people believe they aren't "math people," because they had a bad teacher once. Some people believe they aren't "coders," because they learned in a classroom instead of independently online. People feel trapped somehow by self-imposed limitations that restrict their behaviors. **They know they're in a sandbox, but forget that they can create whatever they want out of the sand.** Play, in all the suggested applications I propose in this book, is a powerful tool in helping us innovate within the sandbox and rediscover our confidence, creative and other.

Play also helps us maximize our learning and stay curious. If we approach our lives with intention to carve out time for play, we'll never be bored or stagnant. We'd be like *that* kid. You know, that annoyingly inquisitive kid who belabors us with incessant questions about why the world is the way that it is and bluntly calls out things that don't make sense…the kid that sometimes catches you off guard and makes you question an assumption you've held forever.

---

14 Ibid.

This book is a cure for becoming a bored and boring adult. So, I found a bunch of non-boring, super interesting adults and young adults, and interviewed them. I consolidated their lessons and advice and framed them under common themes, which I have called Playground Principles. Each principle is named after an item on a playground (e.g. monkey bars, slide, tag...etc.) Each chapter focuses on one Playground Principle, detailing the implications of that form of play and suggesting ways to integrate it into your life.

It's structured a bit like a "choose your own adventure" because everyone knows most books have one bottom line supplemented by hundreds of repetitive examples, so I made my chapters distinct enough so you can jump around freely and learn everywhere.

Play as you would on a playground—if you feel like going on monkey bars, go ahead. If you feel like coloring outside, go ahead! This book is also an opportunity for you to play (with responsible, not reckless, abandon) while you read.

Chapter 1: Recess!

Sets the stage for the book. What recess looks like today and how to create recess time to play in general.

Chapter 2: Slide

Letting go. Thought irrelevance, blowtorching the unnecessary, and mental toughness.

Chapter 3: Pirates on Lava

Magic Realism. Playing pretend, distorting reality to accomplish the impossible, daydreaming, and imagination.

Chapter 4: Digging for Worms

Design Thinking and Scientific Method. How you can play by hypothesizing and experimenting.

Chapter 5: Monkey Bars

Taking Risks. Turning ambition into action, risk-aversion, fighting fears, and taking leaps.

Chapter 6: Tag

Inner Circle. Playing with the people around you. How strong ties and weak ties can positively influence you.

Chapter 7: Color Outside

Interdisciplinarity. Power of making unlikely and unexpected connections.

Chapter 8: On the Field

Activities and Exploration. The creative leverage of activities, specifically sports and travel.

Chapter 9: Sandcastles

Build things. Asset-based mindset. The value of building businesses, hobbies, and skill sets in your free time.

I suggest you start with Chapter 1, just because it lays the foundation by establishing how to create recess time. Feel free to jump around as you desire—you are playing!

Note to my readers: this book is a constant work in progress. I am committed to the scientific method, iteration, and design thinking. Therefore, I welcome and encourage your feedback.

This book is about how we can reinstate recess to preserve our free-spirited and adventurous childhood selves. You will learn how viewing the world like a playground helps you unlock creativity, learn better, and connect meaningfully with ideas and with others.

CHAPTER 1

REINSTATING RECESS

———

"How do we cross the dragon guarding the castle?"

"Trick it by dressing up like another dragon so it doesn't kill you!"

"Throw a shiny diamond far away so it doesn't look at you!"

"Run really, really fast!"

The kids sitting in front of me have bigger things to worry about than our delayed train. They have to form a plan of attack to deceive the spiky, fire-breathing, black-n-red dragon so they can get the treasure in the castle. The girl goes first, surveying the land for secret tunnels and trap doors. But she coughs, and he spots her from the corner of his eye so she stops, drops, and rolls out of sight.

The boy tries to feed the dragon poison berries, but the beast knows better and spits them back in his face. "Ew!" They decide to use their invisibility cloak, the one Harry Potter lent them for this mission, and stay really, *really* quiet. "Shh!" They sneak right by the dragon through the medieval entrance gates. Phew. That was the easy part.

Toes tap on the carpet, diffusing restlessness across the cabin, as parents wait on hold with customer service. *What about our dinner plans? Is the hotel going to give away our room? The weather is terrible. How can the kids enjoy? Why didn't Amtrak tell us we would be delayed? I want my money back.*

I plug my right headphone in to block the boring.

"Attention, ladies and gentlemen! We apologize, but you're next in line to go."

Eyes roll all around.

"Dad, are we *ever* going to leave?"

The dad looks up from his phone, nods, and looks back down. The kid shrugs and returns to the castle, brandishing his pencil sword to intimidate the second dragon, the one guarding the treasure. His brother walkie-talkies him the game plan and the girl, equipped with state-of-the-art binoculars, waits on lookout. The movie gets good.

The engine rumbles the platform and sighs of relief from adults echo in unison, but the kids focus on their goal. The treasure, full of monster trucks and lucky charms and gold coins, glistens in the distance. One, two, three, "Treasure!" and "Break!"

Time to get what they came here for.

The train stood still for three hours, but I guess time goes faster when you're watching a good movie. When I half overheard their dragon adventure, I forgot that we had moved zero feet in two hours. I watched the movie they painted with their words instead of peeping over the Netflix screen of my seat buddy. I couldn't help myself…I just wanted to know how they were so effortlessly able to inject life into dead time.

Wouldn't it be great to embrace boredom? To not have to reach for your headphones or phone in a dull moment to entertain yourself with someone else's life but rather, make your life entertaining in itself? Now, I'm not suggesting we spend all day dreaming about dragons, but instead we can work to mitigate our aversion to "dead time" and develop an affinity for recess.

A CURE TO BOREDOM

I recently got coffee with a friend who uses snapchat prolifically. He happens to be one of my best friends on snapchat, so he sends me everything he does. Literally, every single thing. Here's a snippet from our conversation:

Him: "I went to dinner with Jack and his parents last week—"

Me: "Oh! Il Canale, right? I saw that."

Him: "Yeah, and Jack's mom spilled—"

Me: "Red wine everywhere, and the waiters started singing in Italian, right?"

Him: "Oh yeah. And then the next day, we—"

Me: "Went to karaoke and sang Abba songs, I think."

It took us 15 minutes to start talking about the "unsnappable" things, which incidentally are often not funny or enviable enough to make the snap cut. He started telling me about how he doesn't really feel like himself and hasn't spent time reflecting in a while.

I told him I thought it probably had something to do with his social media use. Does he look at his phone right before going to bed? Right when he wakes up? Does he always have headphones plugged in, blasting music, constantly interfering with thoughts and fuzzing his clear mind? I told him to go for a walk by himself to the monuments (one of the perks of living in Georgetown), and he squirmed at the very idea.

He has a pocket of time unaccounted for and instantly whips out his phone. This compulsive checking and immediate sense of gratification he gets from checking his social media prevents him from using his time to think about tough things, learn something new, or truly relax his mind. Sure, maybe he uses social media to do something productive— and such uses certainly exist. More likely, however, he uses social media to avoid boredom.

I'm a little hesitant to write about boredom because, well, I once took a practice SAT with a reading section about yawning, and that didn't end well. But I'll give it a shot. The concept of boredom has not been around for long. In fact, the word "boredom" was first brought into mainstream vernacular in 1850 by Charles Dickens, in his serial *Bleak House*. People have since studied it in depth, and University of Waterloo psychologist Dr. John Eastwood has dedicated his life to boredom, which he finds exciting.

One of Eastwood's papers, "The Unengaged Mind," defined boredom as "a state in which the sufferer wants to be engaged in some meaningful activity but cannot, characterized by both restlessness and lethargy."[15] Kind of like when you're lying in bed but you want to get up and get food, but you didn't go grocery shopping and, more importantly, don't want to get up. Boredom is essentially that conflict of interest applied to your mind, not just your body. Eastwood says that this application turns out to be an issue of attention. "Which kind of makes sense because attention is the process by which we connect with the world," Eastwood explains.[16]

Today, our attention is spread thin because we connect with the world in so many ways. The problem of experiencing boredom becomes even more severe because we constantly chase not being bored. In Buddhism, the Dharma asserts that the moment we start chasing something, we create its opposite. For example, "right" only exists relative to "left." When we chase happiness, we create the idea of not having

15 Eastwood, John D., Alexandra Frischen, Mark J. Fenske, and Daniel Smilek. 2012. "The Unengaged Mind". *Perspectives On Psychological Science* 7 (5): 482–495. doi:10.1177/1745691612456044.
16 Ibid.

happiness—or sadness.[17] So, when we chase distractions, we become aware of the times distractions are not there, so we become "bored."

For some reason, confessing boredom is like confessing a character flaw. Gayatri Devi, associate English professor at a school in Eastern Pennsylvania, explains why boredom is not as tragic as we make it seem. In fact, unlike work or school, "boredom is our encounter with pure time as form and content."[18] When her students leave campus for the weekend because "campus is boring," she offers them the following advice:

"You know the best antidote to boredom, I asked them? They looked at me expectantly, smartphones dangling from their hands. Think, I told them. *Thinking* is the best antidote to boredom. I am not kidding, kids. Thinking is the best antidote to boredom. Tell yourself, I am bored. Think about that. Isn't that interesting? They looked at me incredulously. Thinking is not how they were brought up to handle boredom."[19]

17 Korda, Josh, About Korda, and Lion's Staff. 2017. "Boredom Is Fascinating – – Josh Korda – Lion's Roar". *Lion's Roar*. Accessed November 7 2018. https://www.lionsroar.com/this-is-how-you-work-with-boredom/.

18 Devi, Gayatri. 2015. "Boredom Is Not A Problem To Be Solved. It's The Last Privilege Of A Free Mind | Gayatri Devi". *The Guardian*. Accessed November 7 2018. https://www.theguardian.com/commentisfree/2015/sep/28/boredom-cures-privilege-free-mind.

19 Ibid.

The kids on the train certainly handled boredom by thinking, and it looked fun. They leaned into boredom to entertain themselves, and in order for us to maximize our learning and preserve our own creativity, we need to do the same.

This isn't a lecture about social media. I use social media, and I know I waste time with my use. But there are advantages to resisting the impulse to grab your phone in a free moment. A big part of increasing your learning potential and making the most of your environment involves shifting your perspective about boredom. It involves seeing free time as an opportunity to grow and change beyond the confines of your nine-to-five job or school day.

Having nothing to do does not have to translate to boredom—it's an opportunity to think. Recess is the time beyond the nine-to-five, the time during which you get to play your way out of boredom.

BEYOND THE 9–5

Sports, music, dance, and other recreational activities used to provide this much-needed break. But even those activities now get twisted into tools of leverage early on, as kids begin training early for college scholarships or professional contracts. Summers become stressful, as the pressure to accumulate relevant work experience seeps earlier and earlier into our personal timeline. While there are still some opportunities to play, like when there's a snow day at school, play time is still often carefully tailored with just the right mix of "break" and "productivity." So it really is no surprise that we no longer know what leisure time really looks like.

According to a 2015 survey conducted by the Bureau of Labor Statistics, the average American over 15 years old spends approximately four hours and 59 minutes per week in "leisure and sports time," and about two hours and 47 minutes of those are spent watching TV. Socializing and communicating hover around 40 minutes, with playing computer games trailing at 25. Sports and recreation would barely win a participation medal, taking up only 18 minutes, but still not the worst. "Relaxing and Thinking" comprises a meager 17 minutes of our free time. And this was in 2015, so it's likely only gotten worse since then.[20]

Recent statistics from the Office for National Statistics show that people under the age of 25 spend anywhere from 29 to 35 percent of their leisure time on screens. The average person has five social media accounts and spends at least two hours per day on them.[21] This adds up to 14 hours a week

20 "American Time Use Survey: Charts By Topic: Leisure And Sports Activities". 2018. *Bls.Gov*. Accessed November 7 2018. https://www.bls.gov/tus/charts/leisure.htm.
21 "Young People Spend A Third Of Their Leisure Time On Devices – Office For National Statistics". 2018. *Ons.Gov.Uk*.

and 728 hours a year. That's 728 hours of watching YouTube fails, crafting the perfect meme to post to your university's ~unrecognized~ meme page or sitting in bed on a Friday night getting FOMO (fear of missing out) and being exposed to secondhand smoke from watching so many Coachella snapchats.

There are two important conclusions to make here. The first is that we all have some allotment of leisure time that we probably choose to occupy poorly. The second is that we are not given a lot of leisure time in the first place, so we have to willingly aggregate moments of boredom and convert them to recess.

So, how do we do that?

REINSTATING RECESS

In 1949, Warren Buffet picked up a book that changed his life. *Security Analysis*, by Columbia professor Benjamin Graham, became Buffet's roadmap. The book was so important that Buffet decided not to make another investing decision until he understood every detail of it.

Accessed November 7 2018. https://www.ons.gov.uk/peoplepopulationandcommunity/leisureandtourism/articles/youngpeoplespendathirdoftheirleisuretimeondevices/2017-12-19.

So, he read it again. And again. And again. He read it 12 times until he understood every detail—only then did he return to investing.[22]

Buffet did not enjoy the book. In fact, reading it over and over again couldn't have been fun. But Buffet chose to embrace the boredom that came along with the book because he knew how important it was. The process, however, was objectively boring.

He had a goal, so he was therefore willing to endure some boring, but necessary, content. Plus, he read this book *during his free time.* He was not required to read it in school, and between his job at his grandfather's grocery store, early business, and investing, he had little time to spare.[23] Yet, he used that time to learn.

Buffet created free time, then created boredom within that free time, because he knew the value of what he was doing. He created recess. Because of this, Buffett was able to maximize his ability to learn and grow by reading books and observing the world around him. Even now, he famously

---

22 "TIP62: WARREN BUFFETT's FAVORITE BOOK, SECURITY ANALYSIS". 2018. *We Study Billionaires.* Accessed November 7 2018. https://www.theinvestorspodcast.com/episodes/ep62-warren-buffetts-favorite-book-security-analysis/.

23 Ibid.

spends 80 percent[24] of his day reading, not because the world has granted him infinite free time, but because he understands how creating recess inspires increased learning.

How do other successful people create recess time and use it to learn? Some popular ways to play:

- Chess: Richard Branson, founder of the Virgin Group, plays chess because he sees "life as one long university education that [he] never had. Every day [he's] learning something new." Chess combines the tactics, bravery, and risk-taking associated with sports, "plus you can have a cup of tea...while you play!"[25]
- Hiking: Jack Dorsey, while running Twitter and FourSquare full time, dedicates each day to a theme. A theme allows him to recall and refocus on the task of the day, without distraction. Saturdays are for hiking.
- Baking: Marissa Mayer, CEO of Yahoo, takes baking to a whole new level. Creating spreadsheets of cupcake and frosting recipes, she loves baking because "it's very scientific." She

---

24 Ward, Marguerite. 2016. "Warren Buffett's Reading Routine Could Make You Smarter, Science Suggests". *CNBC*. Accessed November 7 2018. https://www.cnbc.com/2016/11/16/warren-buffetts-reading-routine-could-make-you-smarter-suggests-science.html.

25 Gillett, Rachel. 2018. "13 Hobbies Highly Successful People Practice In Their Spare Time". *Business Insider*. Accessed November 7 2018. https://www.businessinsider.com/hobbies-highly-successful-people-do-in-their-spare-time-2016-7.

claims baking improves her work because it helps her "come up with new and innovative ways of looking at things."[26]

- Segway Polo: Steve Wozniak enjoys the unlikely combination of polo played on Segways.
- Dinner Parties: Thomas Jefferson, third U.S. president, was famous for his dinner parties. He invited a random assortment of interesting people from various disciplines and posed an interesting philosophical question to them. He knew the random connections you make and the ideas that subsequently arise have immense power.
- Invest in yourself: Dick Costolo, former CEO of Twitter, says that studying improv comedy helped him become a better leader. Emma Watson stayed true to her on-screen counterpart, Hermione, by enrolling at Brown University instead of sitting complacently on her Harry Potter fame.[27]

And there are more. These are just some of the ways successful people spend their free time. They either create pockets of "recess" or use their already free time to learn more, and often what they do in these pockets differentiates them from the rest.

---

26 Ibid.
27 Ibid.

PLAYGROUND PRINCIPLES

Think back to the last time you interacted with a playground, maybe to when you were a kid or last walked by kids playing on a playground. I remember it like this:

I sit impatiently at my desk, staring at the tick of the little hand inch closer to the top of the clock. My friends and I give each other those "race you to the slide!" looks, signaling that the race begins when the bell rings. One minute left. I wiggle my toes in my sneakers to warm them up. Thirty seconds. My heart beats like an artist's hand gripping a pencil, twitching with focused precision. Three, two, one—run.

I sprint to the playground, and my small feet bulldoze through the mulch, creating clouds of dirt and sending wood chips flying all around me. The cool breeze forces my eyes shut for a moment, and in that moment my mind is blank. I jump to grab a monkey bar and flip over and hang upside down. I flip back around and dangle from the precarious height. I extend my arm forward, unsure if I'll make the next bar, but the birds cheer me on so I swing and reach. Swing, reach, swing, reach, until I get to the end. Victorious.

I play tag with my friends. I collect ladybugs. I slide down and climb back up and slide down again. I pretend to steer a ship away from pirates. I forget about time, school, life, and focus on the moment. I play freely.

Playgrounds are really fun. They're places to learn new things, like what happens when you cut an earthworm in half. They're places to bond with strangers over games of hide-and-seek and hopscotch. They're places to test the boundaries of your capabilities and overcome your fears. They are obstacle courses designed to let you play with what I call *responsible abandon*—embracing your free-spirited self with little regard for seriousness beyond basic safety and respect.

Unfortunately, we don't play on playgrounds anymore. As a result, we lose ease of access to the lessons that playgrounds promote. We shove recess into that one box of old childhood things in a corner of the garage, and our neglect forms a layer of dust on our responsible abandon.

So, how do we keep our responsible abandon polished and reap the benefits of play when we no longer have recess?

We view the world like a playground.

I have found that the most successful, creative, and unique people manage to preserve some of that childlike inclination toward play. Play helps them learn more, innovate, and connect better with the world.

I created Playground Principles to help remind us of the lessons we learned while playing as kids. Each principle, inspired by an element of a playground, represents a kind of play. Each chapter zooms in to further explain the perspective behind the principle and provides concrete suggestions for how to implement that form of play.

Together, the Playground Principles help create a mindset and worldview that enables us to not become boring adults but instead reap the benefits of play we ought to have access to.

***

The kids on the train get recess in school. They choose to use that recess however they like. They can swing on the monkey bars, build sandcastles, play tag, or do anything else. They are comfortable with free time and use it to explore. During that recess time they explore things outside what they are taught, play creatively, and become unique.

We all used to have recess in primary school, and we all had it taken away from us one day. I think it's time to reinstate recess.

Let's play.

CHAPTER 2

SLIDE

———

Ninety degrees and blistering sun. Sweat beads drip off her temples, and her muscles pulse, legs tense from stress because 6, 5, 4, 3, 2, 1 chance left to make it, 1 chance left to make her country proud.

The bright sand at the end of the runway draws her eyes, challenging her. *Nobody from your country qualifies. What makes you think you can? 6.70 meters? Ha, I dare you.*

She spits on the ground like a Yankees player, scrapes her rubber soles against the track like a bull ready to charge, and looks straight ahead. Her heart *thump thumps* and her thoughts bounce around like a beam of light in an infinity mirror room, so she takes a deep breath, closes her eyes, makes the sign of the cross, and runs.

Now or never.

She jumps.

The crowd goes wild. Next up, Rio Olympics.

Ivan had plenty of reasons to make excuses. Of the five previous attempts she made, she qualified in two, but someone erased the mark by accident. Both times. Another two were good, just not good enough, and the last was an illegitimate foul. The off-and-on rain didn't help, forcing Ivan to go through several interrupting costume changes during the trial.

She could have freaked out over the weather or the accidental erasing or the false foul, but she didn't. She knew that she couldn't control external circumstances, but she could control her internal thinking. How? She had talked to Ed Tseng, award-winning consultant on peak performance, USTA pro of the year, bestselling author, and my former high school tennis coach. She told the Mexican Olympic Committee that he was as much a part of her success as anyone else, so they flew him to Rio to support her.

What did he teach her?

***

Slide: Letting go. Recognizing how random your thoughts are and knowing you can pick which ones to pay attention to.

You're small, so the slide looks so tall. The ladder seems to reach the clouds, so you better start soon if you want to make it up in time. You climb up, using your hands to grab the next bar, and your feet follow. Then after centuries you make it to the top, glance down at the ground, and sit at the top of the slide. You use your arms to push off the side, propelling yourself forward as you *whoosh* down the slide. No looking back, just letting gravity do its job.

Sliding is about trusting gravity. It's play that encourages you to let go and choose to pay attention to positive thoughts.

Letting go is the primer that allows you to make room to learn and grow. Once you let go, cut out the unnecessary, and break habits, you open yourself up to a whole new world of creative potential.

***

I sat down with Ed at his kitchen table to learn what he did to make such an impact on Ivan. Doodles and macaroni projects from his two toddlers decorated the kitchen in a colorful splatter, and photos of Ed with professional athletes peak out from behind his big red X from his ted talk.

Ed sat with the relaxed but upright posture of a yoga instructor sitting criss-cross, one that reminded me of Siddhartha under the Bodhi tree meditating until he reached enlightenment. His voice was calm like the soothing rhythm of waves gently crashing, and I remembered why I never let the nerves get to me before a tennis match. Ed's comforting presence emits an aura of self-awareness and mind control, so it's only fitting I ask him about letting go.

"Young children are born mentally tough. My daughter, when she was trying to walk, didn't take a couple of steps, fall over, and say, 'Oh man. I didn't walk yesterday either. Maybe I'm not cut out for walking.' She got up and kept going and now she can walk, run, and swim."

I thought about this a bit more. What does a kid think when they fall after trying to walk? Probably nothing. Probably, *oh the ground is cold, let me get up.* Maybe *there's a cookie over there, yum.* We need to look no further than the cute mini-humans ice skating in their marshmallow parkas and earmuffs to see how we're naturally tough.

When kids go ice skating, they don't think about the cold, the ice, or the bruises they get from falling. What do they think about? Probably something like *one foot in front of the other, I probably look like a princess gliding right now, I wonder how fast I can make a lap,* or *I want hot chocolate.* More importantly, they're probably not thinking about their thoughts at all. They're just doing and being. They let go of their thoughts and live in a state of focus, confidence, and motivation.

"It's like holding a tennis ball under water. It takes so much more energy to push down, fighting back buoyancy, than to just let go. When you let go, the ball naturally floats up, bobbing happily atop a crystal blue surface."

I paused for a solid five minutes to think about this and wondered where it went. When was the last time I allowed myself to reset and restore my mind to its default?

"If young children are born resilient, that means we're all born resilient. So where did it go?" I asked Ed, hoping he'd come through with a one, two, three-step elevator pitch to restore your inner resilience in under 30 seconds.

Instead, I got: "As we get older, we're not lacking it. We're just blocking it because we believe our thoughts that seem real."

THOUGHT IRRELEVANCE

I sat at the kitchen table, staring at the Brita filter dripping slowly, overthinking everything I've ever thought, while simultaneously trying to think less.

What do you mean our thoughts aren't real? How do we let go of our thoughts when they appear and disappear at their will?

Enter Subway analogy.

"Imagine you're in a New York City subway station waiting for the C train. Can you control if the A train comes into the station? Or the B train? No. But you can control which train you get on, of course. So you know that if you're waiting for the C train, sometimes the A train is going to come in. But you don't get on the A train because it'll take you for a ride in the wrong direction. So you stay on the platform."

I felt like I was talking to Dumbledore at the end of *Half-Blood Prince* when he purposefully speaks in riddles instead of just straight up telling Harry that a part of his arch nemesis, Voldemort, currently lives inside Harry and that in Harry's quest to destroy Voldemort, he probably will destroy himself.

Ed probably sensed my inner conflict and saw the question on my face because he promptly clarified:

"Here's the thing: A lot of people say you gotta focus. My theory is—we're always focused. But sometimes we're focused on the wrong things. Our thoughts change so quickly, so why do we focus on certain ones over others?"

He's right. Try to remember the last 10 thoughts you had. Can you? I definitely can't.

As the best tennis player (and probably best overall human) in the world, Roger Federer, says "I don't care how positive a person you are, you just see negativity flying all around you and you're like 'I'm down 6–4, I messed up, I should have done this, I should have done that, and now I've just got to get lucky and I'm at the mercy of my opponent.' It's a bad feeling."[28]

Federer is an expert at mental toughness. He doesn't fight the negative thoughts or try to get rid of them. Instead, he accepts and tolerates all the thoughts and emotions that cross his mind, but stays focused on the moment in the game.

I'd like to suggest that our current thoughts matter no more than the thoughts we have while we're asleep.

---

28 "Roger Federer's Mental Secret – Mindfulness-Based Tennis Psychology". 2018. *Mindfulness-Based Tennis Psychology.* Accessed November 7 2018. https://www.tennismentalskills.com/roger-federer-mental-game.

Consider the following situation:

You have a dream tonight. In this dream, I steal your lunch and show up an hour late to our concert date. Would you wake up furious and text me passive aggressive emojis?

I hope not, because whatever you thought happened didn't really happen.

When people have nightmares, they might feel shaken in the morning, but it doesn't take them long to brush it off and move on. Some people have daymares, though, and they let those daymares control their minds.

OUR DEFAULT

Consider the following equations:

$$1+3=4$$

$$15-2=13$$

$$12/6=3$$

$$4+10=14$$

If your initial thought was, *one of these must be incorrect,* you're not wrong. One of them is incorrect. The fact that you likely focused on the one that was incorrect illustrates something psychologists refer to as "negativity bias."

PhD and University of Chicago psychologist John Cacioppo, illustrated negativity bias using pizza and war. He first showed subjects of his study images known to evoke positive feelings, like cars, pizzas, and candy. He then showed them more negative images, like war and death. Last, he showed more neutral images, like plates and hairdryers. As the subjects went through the series of pictures, Cacioppo measured their brain activity.[29]

He observed that the brain reacts more strongly to negative information, and thus concluded that negative information more profoundly impacts our attitude than positive information.[30] We experience this often, when you focus on the one thing you forgot to say in that client meeting instead of all the great things you said or when you remember the one time you got suspended from a tennis match because you flipped off the girls who called your sister *that* word instead

29 "Our Brain's Negative Bias". 2018. *Psychology Today.* Accessed November 7 2018. https://www.psychologytoday.com/us/articles/200306/our-brains-negative-bias.
30 Ibid.

of all the times you exhibited excellent sportsmanship (this may or may not have happened to me.)

Negativity bias is different than being self-critical; certainly, the ability to identify mistakes and critique yourself is extremely important for personal growth and improvement. The difference here is that negativity bias makes your brain disproportionately focus on the negative and obscure the positive.

This makes sense, considering humans have made it this far evolutionarily by avoiding harm. For sake of our survival, we had to be aware of danger and negativity.[31] Our brain has, rightfully so, protected us by developing mechanisms to recognize negativity.

But just because we may be wired to think a certain way does not mean we cannot overcome it.

I like to look at it, as I like to look at most things, with science analogies. Entropy, in simple terms, is loosely defined as disorder of a system. Molecules that are packed tightly together, like those in a block of cheddar cheese, have relatively low entropy compared to molecules in a cheesy sauce.

---

31 "Is Your Negativity Getting In The Way Of Your Creativity?". 2018. *Big Think*. Accessed November 7 2018. https://bigthink.com/good-news-you-can-overcome-negativity-bias.

Melting the cheese into a sauce increases the entropy of the system, because the molecules become more disorderly and have higher energy.

We can track the energy in reactions using energetics (stick with me, I promise there's a point...) There are two main kinds of reactions, endergonic and exergonic. Endergonic reactions are involved in making bonds and require an energy input, whereas exergonic reactions break bonds and release energy. In nature, exergonic reactions are spontaneous; in other words, nature favors breaking things apart.

So, putting things together requires effort and energy.

The Second Law of Thermodynamics states that there is a natural tendency of any isolated system to degenerate into a more disorderly, higher entropy state. This is actually pretty intuitive. For example, ice melts when it's above o degrees Celsius (solid → liquid, low → high entropy!). If you leave an apple alone, it'll decompose and decay (breaking bonds in the apple!). If you stop cleaning your room, your clothes will end up scattered around your floor.

Similarly, if you do nothing to counteract your brain's natural affinity for negativity, you end up focused on the negative.

SELF-IMAGE

As I mentioned earlier, I learned a lot from attending my parents' business conferences. Many people write about the power of words, how the words we say influence our perception of the world, which then influences what actually happens. My dad and his colleagues taught me about this power and having a high self-image from Vern, a stick-figure representing humanity.

I interviewed my dad because not many people can tell this story quite like him.

"Quality of life is directly proportional to self-esteem. A good self-esteem, according to my definition, means that your positive beliefs in your brain exceed the negative beliefs. And a bad self-esteem means that negative beliefs in your brain, about yourself and about the world, exceed the positive beliefs." Which brings us to the question, how to beliefs get into the brain in the first place?

"Well, it's not like the skies part and beliefs come from *heaven*." He laughs to himself, classic Dad. "Beliefs come from listening and associating. The words we say and the words we hear, for example. How we act and how others treat us. Who we encounter and who invests in us. These are all either positive or negative, but in many cases, especially if you don't have the privilege of having a positive childhood, they're usually negative."

He's right. Think about the ratio of good news to bad news you see on TV. Think about the conversations you pretend not to overhear but attentively listen to when waiting in line. I think about how, whenever there is a chance to think out of the box, or do something different, people always talk themselves out of it. Think about your friend who branded herself as a "bad musician" because one person criticized her one time.

"People who don't have the discipline to guard their brain automatically end up with more negative than positive. It's like our garden at home; if we leave it alone, tomatoes, cucumbers, squash…everything dies. But the weeds have no problem peacocking their vibrancy. It's like entropy."

Aha. Yes, that's my DNA right there. Thanks for the nerdiness, Dad!

So, how do we fight entropy?

"You cannot delete what's in your brain, because the mechanism to delete something is to forget, and in order to forget something, you have to remember what you're trying to forget. If someone has a low self-esteem, that means they have a lot more negative than positive in their brain. They can't delete the negative, but they can dilute it."

Enter Vern. A stick figure representing all of humanity.

Below, my sister, Tarika, recreated a picture of Vern,[32] for your reference.[33]

The left side, underneath "Before" shows the default in our brain: more negative than positive. Then, through flooding the brain with positive association and knowledge, the negative gets diluted.

---

32 "Brain PNG – Pluspng". 2018. *Pluspng.* Accessed November 9 2018. http://pluspng.com/brain-png-507.html.
33 "Free Image On Pixabay – Stickman, Stick Figure". 2018. *Pixabay.Com.* Accessed November 9 2018. https://pixabay.com/en/stickman-stick-figure-matchstick-man-151357/.

"The negative never goes away... but you dilute it, and it makes a huge difference. It's like: **A spoon of cyanide can kill you, but if you mix it with 100 gallons of water, it might make you sick, but it won't kill you. There's a big difference between being sick and being dead.**"

Overcoming negative to flood your brain with positive requires breaking habits. Habits are what let defaults be defaults. This next section goes over ways to break the bad habits holding us back.

BREAKING HABITS

"Interlace your fingers."

My right thumb sits comfortably in the gap between my left pointer finger and thumb. My other fingers wedge mechanically, alternating so that my right pinky floats comfortably on the outside.

"Now reverse the order of your thumbs."

I break all the links and put my right thumb over my left, shifting every finger over by one place, but he interrupts me.

"No, just switch the thumbs."

My left thumb forces itself into the pocket between my right thumb and index finger, squishing awkwardly like a large person on a slightly-too-small economy seat. Nothing wrong with being there, but it makes things a tad too tight.

"Now cross your arms."

Right arm over left and left hand on right bicep. Clockwork.

Switch it? Simple enough.

I separate my arms, do a little disco roll, and end up in the same orientation as before. Two-seconds-too-long later, I finally manage to switch my arms. I feel off-balanced...as if one side of my body is heavier than the other.

"I just asked you to break a simple physiological habit. Imagine a more complex habit and a change like 'be creative.'"

In his class, Creativity in Imagination, Robert Bies challenges his students to break habits that limit their imagination. This activity is one of the many unique tasks he asks his students to perform. Some other things include screaming really loudly somewhere on campus, going to a public place with a group and asking them to freeze for two minutes, and abandoning students outdoors with a few tools and seeing what they come up with.

I talked to a student in his class, Katie Rogers, who sent me an email about her experience with some of these tasks. The email reads,

I am typically pretty quiet in public scenarios and hate having attention drawn to me, so this assignment was terrifying for me. It took me awhile to even build up the courage to decide what I would do. Getting myself to complete the challenge was difficult, but once I did it, I felt incredibly relived and even proud of myself. I think that we are trained to conform to societal norms, which is why breaking from these norms can be so hard. After this assignment, I really thought a lot about why people behave the way that they do, and why it can be so hard to break out of these norms. It definitely made me pay more attention to my own behaviors and made me a little more willing to be more "out there" than before.

Robert makes students do this because he wants them to test the limits they impose upon themselves. We are habitually trained to seek comfort over creativity, and we're attached to habits that hold us back.

There's a lot of information out there about how to cultivate good habits and break bad ones. Robert wants us to break the habits that hold us back from being creative, and Vern wants us to break the habits that contribute to the negative in our brain.

To do both, I offer a strategy I learned in creative writing class: *Blowtorch.*

BREAK HABITS WITH A BLOWTORCH

I handed in my paper, margins one inch on each side, paragraph formatting, 1.5 spaced, Times New Roman, stapled carefully at the top left corner just as I handed in all my other papers. I proofread it a million times, referenced literary themes with nuance, and organized my story much like I organized any essay—outlining it so that there was a logical flow and hand-picking every detail until they all combined beautifully to form a conclusion.

I was confident in my writing skills, as every teacher until 11th grade shaped me into the analytical writer I was then. So, why should my creative writing class have been any different?

When I got back my paper, or what was left of it, I flipped through the pages looking for a grade. No grade. Instead, huge chunks of sentences, even paragraphs, were crossed out with purple Crayola marker. Exclamation points, question marks, tildes, and emoji faces lined the margins, arrows nonsensically connected disparate parts of my story, and the word *blowtorch* was scribbled everywhere.

Who grades papers with Crayola markers? Clearly, I was taking a class with some sort of lunatic, and so I demanded justice.

I met with Q, posture tall and opening statement memorized. I began to make my case, and he smirked.

"Try less."

Ouch. My ego recoiled and my tongue froze.

"You have to blowtorch all this stuff—this stuff that's just there to sound good. You're telling me a story, so tell it. I don't want all this dog poop."

Ouch, again.

Bruised, I quickly learned how to blowtorch by careful observation and focusing on the core, the bare minimum, of the stories around me. Living in the moment allowed my inner voice to seep through the gaps neglected by thesis statements and semicolons.

Blowtorching means detaching from what you currently have to make space for something better. It means cutting out the excess—anything that doesn't feel genuine and tries too hard to tell your story. It means trying less and letting go, so your story can tell itself.

The point here is that you can use blowtorching as a way to break bad habits and let go of the negative thoughts that are unnecessary "dog poop" in your life.

These are some things to think about while blowtorching your way out of bad habits:

1. What are you attached to and why?
2. Are any of these things holding you back in any way?
3. What is your core narrative? What is the bare minimum you need to tell that story?
4. Cut something out. Most of the time, after the cut is made, you won't even remember what you lost.

Blowtorching is a kind of play that helps you learn more, cut out fluff, and do things you didn't think you could do. For me, writing is one of the best ways to visualize blowtorching. You start typing away, thinking everything you write is gold. But if you detach from your words to rearrange and delete things, you end up with unlikely combinations and creative opportunities.

This playground principle, *Slide*, helps us detach from negative thoughts, counter our default mental programming, and break habits that limit us.

***

Rio.

Ed was hanging with athletes in the Olympic Village, all of whom qualified to be where they are. They were stressed out, and Ivan was no exception. He could sense her tension and took her out to dinner.

He told her, "I know you're stressed about how your legs feel. You're tight. You haven't been sleeping, tossing and turning. You have to compete in a few days...but to be honest with you, a couple nights of lost sleep and being tight don't have to affect your performance."

As soon as he said that, he could see the relief wash over her face. The next morning, he got a text from her saying she slept like a baby.

Ivan stopped focusing on what was wrong and worrying about her preparedness; instead, she let herself relax.

When she remembered the subway analogy and importance of thought irrelevance, her thinking and body relaxed.

She fought entropy and negative bias by remembering that she can choose any of the infinite perspectives to believe, so she flooded her head with positivity.

She blowtorched all the thoughts that weren't absolutely critical for her to jump well. Although she had a habit of letting her lack of sleep interfere with her performance, she broke it to defy her limits.

Only after remembering to *slide* could Ivan jump to her best potential.

CHAPTER 3

PIRATES ON LAVA

———

When I walked into the trendy New York City coffee shop earlier that day, I was prepared to for the interview with a guy my dad knew and told me to meet. When I stalked him on LinkedIn, I saw that he had a lot of banking experience and had started several companies. I expected to see an uptight, fast-paced New Yorker charge through the door, time-bound by his Google calendar. I waited a few moments, and dozens of those characters shuffled in and out without stopping.

"Devika?"

I turned around to see a man in a scarf, kind of like my fourth-grade art teacher, with curly hair and baggy pants. He started asking me what my book was about, and I told him it's still in the "early stages," but I'm interested in learning about how to preserve creativity in a world that tries to destroy it. I wanted to know how to maximize beyond-the-nine-to-five learning.

What I didn't see on his LinkedIn was that he was the author of a superhero fantasy book, *Bioman*, and hasn't worked in the private sector for years. Instead, he's now dedicated his life to screenwriting, with a side of managing a few companies here and there.

Alfie grew up in the UK before doing his undergrad and PhD in physics at St. Andrews. He then started working for a fintech company in Cambridge before moving to Japan for a year to work for Tokyo Mitsubishi Bank. Then he shipped himself to Australia in 2000 to work for another fintech company before arriving in NYC in 2001 to begin building his credibility as a consultant.

This man was all over the place, and he still hadn't mentioned his book or his screenwriting.

"My first girlfriend got me into screenwriting." Of course, it's always a girl. "Her dad wrote *Elephant Man*."

He then wrote his first script, which of course did not get any traction. But as he progressed through his professional career, screenwriting remained a sort of backdrop for him.

"So I spent the next 15 years studying the art and craft of screenwriting while I was going around the world deploying weapons of mass financial destruction."

I wanted to know how Alfie preserved his creativity and rediscovered the potential of his imagination after working for 25 years in the private sector.

Alfie stays creative by dreaming.

***

Pirates on Lava: Playing by daydreaming. Realizing that you can spin reality by making space to imagine and daydream and that you can learn a lot from playing pretend.

Playgrounds usually have some kind of treehouse. When I was younger, my sisters and I thought of it as a pirate ship.

"Ahoy, go lurk over yonder through the telescope. Do you see the enemies?"

I stood atop the clubhouse, steering the ship and delegating work to my crew. My youngest sister ran the engine, swinging back and forth on the swing at a steady rate to propel our ship's motor. My middle sister was on lookout, in charge of pressing the panic button if the enemies pointed their cannons at us.

The waves rocked the ship left and right, we lost our balance, and slipped. Oh no! Man overboard! Release the life raft, quick, before the enemies take her hostage.

Playing pretend didn't feel like playing pretend. In those moments, we were pirates, and our reality was our experience on the pirate ship.

Exercising our imaginations through daydreaming can teach us a lot about the world around us. It can allow our minds to generate new and clever ideas. Imagination lets us construct our own reality and therefore see the world and approach problems from different angles.

Playing pretend allows us to redefine the impossible.

***

SUBJECTIVE REALITY

In a two part-episode of *Star Trek*, entitled "The Menagerie," the crew finds a new planet called Talos. The inhabitants of Talos create virtual realities in the minds of other people. Bud Tribble, one of the key software developers for Apple's original Macintosh computer, used this concept of a *reality distortion field* to explain how Steve Jobs could convince anyone of anything. In fact, when Andy Hertzfeld joined Apple and learned they were to ship the first Macintosh software within the next 10 months, he thought it was impossible—until he saw it for himself.[34]

Andy explained his discovery and reluctance to accept the alternative reality in a blog post he wrote, explaining a conversation he had with Bud.

"Bud, that's crazy!" I told him. "We've hardly even started yet. There's no way we can get it done by then."

"I know," he responded in a low voice, almost a whisper.

"You know? If you know the schedule is off base, why don't you correct it?"

"Well, it's Steve. Steve insists that we're shipping in early 1982 and won't accept answers to the contrary. The best way to describe the situation is a term from Star Trek. Steve has a reality distortion field."

"A what?"

"A reality distortion field. In his presence, reality is malleable. He can convince anyone of practically anything. It wears off

---

34 Hertzfeld, Andy, Steve Capps, Donn Denman, Bruce Horn, and Susan Kare. n.d. *Revolution In The Valley*.

when he's not around, but it makes it hard to have realistic schedules. And there's a couple of other things you should know about working with Steve."

"What else?"

"Well, just because he tells you that something is awful or great doesn't necessarily mean he'll feel that way tomorrow. You have to low-pass filter his input. And then, he's really funny about ideas. If you tell him a new idea, he'll usually tell you he thinks it's stupid. But then, if he actually likes it, exactly one week later, he'll come back to you and propose your idea to you, as if he thought of it."[35]

Andy didn't buy the whole reality distortion mumbo jumbo, but as an Apple employee, it was only a matter of time before he saw it for himself.

"The reality distortion field was a confounding mélange of a charismatic rhetorical style, an indomitable will, and an eagerness to bend any fact to fit the purpose at hand. Amazingly, the reality distortion field seemed to be effective even if you were acutely aware of it, although the effects would fade after Steve departed. We would often discuss potential

---

35 Hertzfeld, Andy, Steve Capps, Donn Denman, Bruce Horn, and Susan Kare. n.d. *Revolution In The Valley.*

techniques for grounding it, but after a while most of us gave up, accepting it as a force of nature."[36]

Techopedia defines Reality Distortion Field as follows: "a phenomenon in which an individual's intellectual abilities, persuasion skills and persistence make other people believe in the possibility of achieving very difficult tasks."[37]

Steve Jobs used his RDF to bend reality to make an impossible task seem possible and even easy. He used RDFs to inspire his employees and motivate them to overcome whatever hurdles were necessary to accomplish the goal. Jobs was unique because his charisma convinced others to delude themselves into integrating the otherwise "impossible" into the conceivable.

And Apple isn't the only company that uses imagination deliberately to unlock creativity and access the impossible. Tesla and Elon Musk also distort reality to make way for the exceptional. As early SpaceX engineer Kevin Brogan explains, "Elon Musk doesn't say, 'You have to do this by 2 p.m. on

---

36 "How Steve Jobs Created The Reality Distortion Field (And You Can, Too)". 2016. *Medium*. Accessed November 8 2018. https://medium. com/@jhargrave/how-steve-jobs-created-the-reality-distortion-field-and-you-can-too-4ba87781adba.

37 "What Is A Reality Distortion Field? – Definition From Techopedia". 2018. *Techopedia.Com. Accessed November 9 2018*. https://www.techopedia.com/definition/23694/reality-distortion-field-rdf.

Friday.' Instead, he says, 'I need the impossible done by Friday at 2 p.m. Can you do it?'"

"Then, when you say yes, you're not working hard because he told you to. You're working hard for yourself." [38]

Because of this culture, the team at SpaceX built rocket computing systems for around $10,000, when the norm was over $10 million. When traditional manufacturers sent them quotes, they built parts on budgets that were one-twentieth of those quotes.[39] In order to accomplish these goals, Elon Musk plays with his imagination to distort his perception of reality. In doing so, he and his team are able to test the limits of what is practically conceivable to achieve things nobody can even imagine.

While not all of us may go on to launch rockets, build hyper loops, or make iPhones, we can certainly learn from RDFs.

We all have our own reality distortion fields. Yours is operating right now; it is the reality you project to the world about yourself. It defines your abilities, strengths, limitations, preferences, and pretty much anything else anyone notices about

---

38 D'Onfro, Jillian. 2018. "The 'Absolute Worst Thing' Spacex Employees Can Say To Elon Musk ". *Business Insider.* Accessed November 8 2018. https://www.businessinsider.com/ elon-musk-doesnt-believe-in-impossible-2015-5.

39 Ibid.

you. What you perceive yourself as becomes actual reality. When you believe something about yourself, others believe it. "And when you get down to it, that's all that's required for reality—that we all believe it."[40]

EMBELLISHING YOUR RDF

For Jobs, expansive RDF enabled a change in the course of computer history with a fraction of the resources of IBM or XEROX. As Debi Coleman, an early Apple employee, remarks, "It was a self-fulfilling distortion. You did the impossible because you didn't realize it was impossible."[41]

And here we arrive at an exciting opportunity. **If we can change the way we see reality, if we can integrate some more fantasy into our perspective, we can accomplish things we didn't know were possible.**

If we want, we can learn an absurd amount of information in a short period of time or complete extreme physical tasks, simply by performing small acts of self-delusion.

Let's take a look at one of my favorite books: *El Ingenioso Don Quixote de la Mancha*. In case you are not familiar

---

40 Hertzfeld, Andy, Steve Capps, Donn Denman, Bruce Horn, and Susan Kare. n.d. *Revolution In The Valley*.

41 Johnson, Craig E, and Michael Z Hackman. 2013. *Leadership*.

(read it after you finish this), the novel was written by Miguel de Cervantes in 1615. A satire against the chivalric *caballero* stories of knights and damsels then in literary vogue, the story follows Don Quixote, a man who reads books into madness.[42]

Obsessed with these romantic and, well, quixotic, stories, Quixote becomes a self-proclaimed knight and sets out into the world to emulate his literary role models.

How did he become the knight he imagined himself to be? I'll tell you a little about his story.

Essentially, while digging through storage, Quixote found some rusty armor that belonged to his ancestors. The equipment was intact, although the helmet had no visor protecting the face. No matter, he quickly fashioned another out of strip pieces of stiff paper and iron. To Quixote, "it was the most magnificent helmet to ever exist."

Quixote's horse, Rocinante, looked more like a donkey than a horse, but Quixote saw him as the most magnificent horse of all time.

---

42 "Historical Context For Don Quixote By Miguel De Cervantes | The Core Curriculum". 2018. *College.Columbia.Edu*. Accessed November 8 2018. https://www.college.columbia.edu/core/node/1764.

Equipped with armor and a steed, Quixote blazed forward, eager to rid the world of injustice and perform the great deeds of a knight.

Everything Quixote saw was as fantastic as how he had read. When he approached a plain inn, he saw a gleaming castle with turrets thrusting to the sky, a moat, a drawbridge, and all other castle-related paraphernalia. When he ate a meal of dry fish and moldy bread, he was convinced it was gourmet.

My favorite of his adventures, probably his most famous one, is the one with the windmills. One day, Don Quixote and his squire, Sancho, while crossing the plane of Montiel, caught sight of dozens of windmills. Translated[43] (by me), their conversation goes something like this:

"There stands more than 30 terrible giants. I will fight them and kill them all, and we shall make ourselves rich with the spoils."

"What giants?" Sancho asks.

"Those, there with the long arms," responded Quixote.

"Those are not giants, but windmills."

---

43 El Ingenioso Hidalgo De Don Quijote De La Mancha. Capítulo IV". 2018. Elmundo.Es. Accessed November 22 2018. https://www.elmundo.es/quijote/capitulo.html?cual=4

"If you are afraid, then go say your prayers, but I shall fight them."

Quixote charged forward, yelling threats at the giants. A slight wind sent the giants propelling their arms like helicopters, but Quixote charged forward. His sword pierced one of the sails and wrenched him forward with such force that he and Rocinante lay motionless on the ground.

"Didn't I warn your worship that they were windmills?" reminds Sancho.

"I believe that some evil enchanter turned the giants into windmills to rob me of a glorious victory."

Quixote then went on to perform more good deeds and defeat more evil. Regardless of how frequently and forcefully Sancho tried to make Quixote see reality as it was, Quixote paid no attention. He continued to live in his self-fashioned reality and eventually became famous for his stories throughout the land.

Even though most people see Quixote as a representation of the hopelessness of trying to live up the *caballero* ideals, I think there's something quite admirable about Quixote, something we can learn from.

Now, I don't suggest that we all read Harry Potter and then believe we are wizards and relinquish reality as a result. Rather, I think we can learn something from Quixote's RDF.

He changed his RDF so he could believe he was a knight, so the world could see him as a knight. While he may not have defeated real giants, he brought a sense of accomplishment to his life.

Stories like these are common in Spanish Literature, specifically during the Magic Realism phenomenon of the twentieth century. For reference, Magic Realism strives to invigorate the ordinary with fantastical elements, unlike pure fantasy, which seeks to transport to a completely different world.

It is important to know that even though magic realism is characterized by fantastic plots and magical elements, the genre was never meant to be escapist. Instead, these others sought to occupy the special space between dreams and reality—a place in which we live every moment yet still can neither name nor reconcile.

DAYDREAM TO DIY MAGIC REALISM

"The whole theory of relativity was Einstein just daydreaming," Alfie Rustom, former banker and current superhero screenwriter, tells me.

As a kid, Alfie lived in a hybrid world of sci-fi and reality. He read a book a day and immersed himself so deeply in fantastical worlds that he started to become depressed because his "ordinary life was simply not up to par."

What was the solution?

"I stepped away from fantasy to start creating a magical life for myself."

So, how did Alfie "create a magical life" for himself?

He dreams intentionally during the day. Doing so expands his RDF and brings a sense of magic realism into his life— two things that, as we've seen, definitely make someone more creative.

What is an ex-banker, serial entrepreneur, fantasy-whiz, superhero screenwriter's creative process?

It depends. If he's "doing some serious imagining," he plugs his earphones in and lets his imagination just wander.

"When you're daydreaming, it's more like chiseling away a block of stone piece by piece consciously, but not deciding what the sculpture becomes until the end. Instead, you sort of let it tell you what it is creating."

I didn't buy it at all. In fact, I thought this was just some artsy thing that I'd never understand, like Oscar films or modern art. But then, I tried it.

And it still didn't work.

The sun was out, its hot rays beating down, stinging my skin. Perfect day for a run, so I ran to the monuments and sat on the stairs in front of Abe. I had just re-listened to Alfie's interview, so I thought I'd give this whole daydreaming thing a shot.

At first, I was confused about where to look. Was I supposed to stare into the distance? Close my eyes? I tried focusing on the Washington Memorial, but all the people moving around in the periphery kept stealing my attention. Then I tried closing my eyes, but the darkness was daunting. What was I supposed to think of? The options were too plentiful, and I was immediately overwhelmed.

So, I did what I always do when I'm lost, and I turned to science.

Cognitive scientists hypothesize that our ability to imagine is the result of a neural network that coordinates activity across several regions of the brain, named the "mental workplace." In a study conducted at Dartmouth, PHD Alex

Schlegal measured the brain activity in 15 participants whom he asked to look at and recall pictures of abstract shapes. While recalling, participants were asked to either recall the exact shape or modify it to a new shape.[44]

Alex and his team hypothesized that the fMRI scans would show use of the visual cortex because that part of the brain processes imagery. They found, however, that in addition to activating the visual cortex, the mental manipulation activated twelve other "regions of interest." Schlegal concluded that many areas in the brain work together when we imagine.[45]

Daydreaming allows us to give our minds a break—to let them wander and release, and to activate our "mental workspace." In his book *Tinker Dabble Doodle Try*, Harvard MD and CEO of the NeuroBusiness group Srini Pillay argues that positive constructive daydreaming, or PCD, helps unleash the imagination. He offers the following steps to proactively daydream:

1. Start by planning. While this may sound counterintuitive, "Just think of it as taking the time to plan a skydive rather than spontaneously jumping out of an airplane."

---

44 Ferro, Shaunacy. 2018. "How Imagination Works". *Popsci.Com*. https://www.popsci.com/science/article/2013–09/how-imagination-works.
45 Ibid.

2. Turn your attention inward. Most of what we learn comes from the outside because most of our time is spent engaging with our surrounding world. We're now trying to learn from ourselves, so actively look inward.

3. Do something low-key. Studies show that mind-wandering activities can facilitate creative incubation. Try knitting, coloring, or doodling to "get your creative brain charged."

4. Overcome the gut response. Apparently, we're wired to associate our own creativity with agony. Creativity might make you feel queasy at first, but that's normal.[46]

Daydreaming is a really fun way to play and a great way to generate innovative ideas. The next section brings up several notable examples of people who have daydreamed their way to invention.

DAYDREAM TO INNOVATE

Some of the most successful innovators in the arts, sciences, and business worlds are adept daydreamers. Christopher Nolan thought of the idea for *Inception* after having a particularly lucid dream. Andrew Stanton thought of the idea for *WALL-E* while at a baseball game, binoculars in hand.[47]

---

46 Pillay, Srinivasan S. n.d. *Tinker Dabble Doodle Try.*
47 Davis, Jeffrey. 2018. "The Science Of The Daydreaming Paradox For Innovation". *Psychology Today.* https://www.psychologytoday.com/us/blog/tracking-wonder/201708/the-science-the-daydreaming-paradox-innovation.

My favorite example is 3M's Arthur Fry's invention of the post-it note. In the early 1970s, Fry used to sing in his church choir. But whenever he stood and opened his hymnal to sing, the paper bookmarks he used to mark songs always slipped out of his book. During a rather boring sermon, Fry's mind wandered back to a lecture he attended once, in which Spencer Silver, serial inventor, developed a high quality but "low-tack" adhesive that was strong enough to hold papers together but weak enough to pull them apart without tearing. In that moment of wandering, Fry realized that Silver's reusable adhesive would provide his bookmarks with exactly the right temporary anchoring he needed.[48]

And now we have Post-it ® Notes.

Jonah Lehrer, author of Imagine: How Creativity Works, said the following about Fry's invention:

"It's not an accident that Arthur Fry was daydreaming when he came up with the idea for a sticky bookmark...A more disciplined thought process wouldn't have made the connection between the annoying little pieces of paper he used to bookmark his choir music and a weak adhesive another 3M

---

48 Bellis, Mary. 2017. "Meet Arthur Fry: Inventor Of The Post-It Note". 2018. *Thoughtco.* Accessed November 8 2018. https://www.thoughtco. com/history-of-post-it-note-199232

engineer had developed. The errant daydream is what made Post-it notes possible."[49]

Lehrer explains how neuroscientists have discovered that we're most creative when we're not trying to think creatively. In short, they have observed that when the mind wanders, the right hemisphere of the brain makes connections between seemingly unrelated things, connections which then become sudden insights and "aha" moments.[50]

An important thing to note here is that there is a right and wrong way to daydream. The trick is finding a dynamic equilibrium between letting your mind wander and remaining aware enough to recognize a creative moment when it appears. In other words, not all daydreams are equal.

Lehrer notes that "the reason Fry is such a good inventor— he has more than 20 patents to his name, in addition to Post-it Notes—isn't simply that he's a prolific mind-wanderer. It's that he's able to pay attention to his daydreams and to detect those moments when his daydreams generate insights."[51]

Creativity happens when you deliberately daydream.

49 Lehrer, Jonah. 2012. *Imagine*. [Grand Haven, MI]: Brilliance Audio.
50 Ibid.
51 Ibid.

Jonathan Schooler, a researcher who has pioneered the study of daydreaming, takes a daydreaming walk every day. He suggests meditation, long showers, games of ping pong, coloring, and other things that allow your mind to wander within the constraints of a semi-focused activity.[52]

Take some recess time to deliberately daydream. You'll be able to play with your RDF, experiment with ways of seeing the world, and let your mind wander to find discovery.

***

My favorite quote from Don Quixote is copied below, in its original Spanish and translated to English:

Don Quixote soy, y mi profesión la de andante caballería. Son mis leyes, el deshacer entuertos, prodigar el bien y evitar el mal. Huyo de la vida regalada, de la ambición y la hipocresía, y busco para mi propia gloria la senda más angosta y difícil. ¿Es eso, de tonto y mentecato?[53]

or

---

52 Mooneyham, Benjamin W., and Jonathan W. Schooler. 2013. "The Costs And Benefits Of Mind-Wandering: A Review.". *Canadian Journal Of Experimental Psychology/Revue Canadienne De Psychologie Expérimentale* 67 (1): 11–18. doi:10.1037/a0031569.
53 05, Capítulo. 2015. "Capítulo 05". Donquijotedelamanchadecervantes. Blogspot.Com. Accessed November 22 2018. http://donquijotedelamanchadecervantes.blogspot.com/2015/03/capitulo-05.html.

I am Don Quixote, and my profession is that of a knight-er-
ranty. These are my laws, to undo wrongs, and to lavish good
and relinquish evil. I flee from the gift of life, from ambition
and hypocrisy, and I see my own glory in the narrowest and
most difficult path. Is that stupid and silly?

CHAPTER 4

DIGGING FOR WORMS

———

Spiral staircases and techy interfaces loom over me as I walk through the aisles of the new Amazon Books store on M Street, hoping inspiration will stop me in my tracks. The futuristic aisles distract me from my mission, and I dismiss cover after cover as cliché, grotesque, or meaningless.

Blank white. A boring (or classic) look only Malcolm Gladwell can pull off.

Way-too-literal personification. Obvious, give your reader some credit.

Random colors and graphics throw excitement at me before the story can speak for itself. Don't try so hard.

Just as I turn toward the door, defeated, inspiration smacks me in the face. A simple story hook, line, sinks the corner of my eye and reels me in to learn more.

Teal brushstrokes somewhat haphazardly strewn about the white cover, like carefree finger-painting, frame it in a warm, kindergarten nostalgia. The title is written in scribbles etched on a chalkboard, back when people used chalkboards, a little slanted because thoughts don't happen in straight lines.

Creative Confidence: Unleashing the Creative Potential Within Us All by Tom and David Kelley (genius brothers in innovation; David founded IDEO) is exactly that kind of playful attraction I want my book to have. I bought it, read it, read it again, and in it, finally found the words to describe a passion I've had for the longest time: Design Thinking.

In the book, the brothers tell a story about a man named Doug Dietz. Doug worked for General Electric Healthcare for twenty years designing large medical imaging devices. One of his proudest designs was a magnetic resonance imaging (MRI) machine that was so special it had been submitted for an International Design Excellence Award.[54]

---

54 Kelley, Tom, and David Kelley. 2015. *Creative Confidence*. London: William Collins.

But one day, when he was observing his prized design in action, he saw a little girl heading toward the room with her parents. He saw her cry on her way to the scanner he designed and learned upon later inquiry that approximately 80 percent of children had to be sedated before entering the MRI machine.[55]

As David Kelley remarks in his Ted Talk, "He was saving lives but scaring kids."[56]

How was he going to redesign the experience for the kids?

This brings us to this chapter's highlighted playground principle—digging for worms.

***

Digging for Worms: Investigation. Taking a field of dirt and digging mercilessly until you find squirmy worms and sticks and pebbles you didn't know you'd find and use them to make something cool.

---

55 Ibid.
56 Kelley, David. 2018. "How To Build Your Creative Confidence". *Ted. Com.* Accessed November 8 2018. https://www.ted.com/talks/david_ kelley_how_to_build_your_creative_confidence?language=en.

Digging for worms refers to committing to the process of experimentation using the scientific method and design thinking principles—testing hypotheses, collaborating on processes and prototypes, getting feedback, and repeating until you've done something that adds value to your intended recipient.

Taking recess time to just dig for worms is structured play that makes use of your RDF (chapter 3) to exercise your mind methodically.

Learning to dig for worms assuages our fear of judgement and failure by boosting our creative confidence. When we commit to experimenting, we care less about results.

***

Doug knew he needed to make a change. He knew he wouldn't have been able to secure enough funding to redesign a new machine from scratch, so he enrolled in an executive education course at Stanford d. school (design school) and learned about design thinking.

Design thinking, as defined by Tim Brown, CEO of IDEO, the world's leading innovation and design firm, is "a human-centered approach to innovation that draws from the designer's toolkit to integrate the needs of the people, the possibilities of technology, and the requirement of business success."[57]

When Doug designed his MRI machine the first time, he didn't focus on the user experience. This time around, post d. school, Doug started observing children at a day care center. He spoke to specialists to understand the experience of young patients. He shared his problem with those around him—experts from a children's museum, pediatricians, and consultants—who were not included in the conversation the first time.[58]

After learning about the client experience, Doug was determined to make his machines more enjoyable for kids.

Design thinking tools helped him transform the dreary MRI experience into an adventure story with colorful decals, paint and even a script that a "narrator" could read.[59]

57 "Design Thinking: A Method for Creative Problem Solving". 2018. *IDEO U.* Accessed November 8 2018. https://www.ideou.com/pages/design-thinking.

58 Kelley, Tom, and David Kelley. 2013 "Slate's Use Of Your Data". 2018. *Slate Magazine.* Accessed November 8 2018. https://slate.com/human-interest/2013/10/creative-confidence-a-new-book-from-ideos-tom-and-david-kelley.html.

59 Kelley, Tom, and David Kelley. 2015. *Creative Confidence.* London: William Collins.

Some of his ideas included a pirate ship with a steering wheel, the chance to pick a toy from a treasure chest at the end, a space ship that repurposed the dreadful MRI sound into a "takeoff" sound, and a "coral city" underwater adventure.[60]

The design thinking process enabled Doug to discover an innovative solution to his problem.

In general, when designing products or consulting a client, **design-thinking can be a really useful tool in coming up with original ideas, creating products that consumers actually need and use, and pushing the bounds of the "possible" just a little further.**

Luckily, the process is broken down into simple, easy-to-learn steps.

DESIGN THINKING STEPS

According to IDEO, there are three essential aspects of Design Thinking:

- Empathy
- Ideation
- Experimentation

---

60 Ibid.

EMPATHY

"When we think about design thinking, the first word that comes to mind is human."[61]

Design thinkers focus on the *people* they are designing for so they can generate human-centered products. They generate empathy for their clients, which they can't do from behind a desk. They actually leave to get to know their clients on a personal level.

Empathy is all about humbling yourself to focus on the needs of those you are serving, which requires real fieldwork. Consider the series of events about a group of students who took the Extreme Affordability class taught by Stanford professor Jim Patell.

Assignment: Design a low-cost incubator for newborn babies in the developing world.[62]

A group of computer scientists, engineers, and business students realized they couldn't effectively design for a customer

61 "What Is Design Thinking?". 2018. *IDEO U*. Accessed November 8 2018. https://www.ideou.com/blogs/inspiration/what-is-design-thinking.

62 Routson, Joyce. 2011. "Embracing A Way To Change The World". 2018. *Stanford Graduate School Of Business*. Accessed November 8 2018. https://www.gsb.stanford.edu/insights/embracing-way-change-world.

they didn't know, especially from a cushy cafe in suburban California.

So, they packed their bags and headed to Nepal, where they spoke with families and doctors in person to understand their needs. They realized that the Nepalese villagers didn't need a cheaper incubator in the hospitals because the babies that were in most danger were the ones born prematurely far from hospitals. Instead, they needed a way to keep babies without access to incubators warm.[63]

This research—that they only could have gotten through first-hand fieldwork—led them to design a special "sleeping bag" known as the Embrace Infant Warmer. It costs considerably less than an incubator and has the potential to save millions of babies every year.[64]

None of this would have happened if that team hadn't made the effort to bridge the gap between producer and consumer by building empathy.

When digging for worms, empathy happens when you put down your fancy shovel, get a little mud on your jeans, and ground yourself to the most personal level.

---

63 Ibid.
64 Ibid.

IDEATION

Pretty much what it sounds like. Brainstorming—generating lots of ideas. The purpose is to generate ideas quickly, overcome thought blocks, broaden the horizon of perspective, and build enthusiasm.

IDEO has seven rules when it comes to running brainstorms:

1. Defer judgement
2. Encourage wild ideas
3. Build on the ideas of others
4. Stay focused on the topic
5. One conversation at a time
6. Be visual
7. Go for quantity[65]

A big part of ideation involves getting rid of the fear of being judged. In his article about reclaiming creative confidence, Tom Kelley says the following about this fear:

"Most of us accept that when we are learning, say, to ski, others will see us fall down until practice pays off. But we can't risk our business-world ego in the same way. As a result, we self-edit, killing potentially creative ideas because we're

---

65 Ahmed, Muneer. 2011. "Openideo - 7 Tips On Better Brainstorming". *Challenges.Openideo.Com*. Accessed November 8 2018. https://challenges.openideo.com/blog/seven-tips-on-better-brainstorming.

afraid… But you can't be creative if you are constantly censoring yourself."[66]

Ideation helps to extract as many ideas as possible. A big part of ideation involves capturing the thoughts that run aimlessly through your head in some kind of an idea notebook. Write them all down—even the ones that sound crazy—because those are often the game-changers.

Here's an example of ideation:

When IDEO worked with Air New Zealand to improve customer experience, they started with a brainstorming workshop intended to breed crazy ideas. Ideas like harnesses to hold standing people, hammocks, and bunk beds were thrown around the room—a creative process that led to a breakthrough idea. The Skycouch is a lie-flat seat for the economy class.[67] (If you ask me, they should have called it the Skycoach or the CoachCouch, but that's just one self-proclaimed pun-master's opinion.)

It seemed impossible to create a couch in economy seats without taking up more space, but the designers created a "heavily

---

66 Kelley, Tom, and David Kelley. 2012 "Reclaim Your Creative Confidence". 2012. *Harvard Business Review*. Accessed November 8 2018. https://hbr.org/2012/12/reclaim-your-creative-confidence.
67 Ibid.

padded section [that] swings up like a footrest to transform an airline row into a futon-like platform."[68]

The IDEO/Airline team likely would not have thought up this idea without a quantity-over-quality approach to brainstorming. **Nobody was scared of being judged because they knew that generating as many ideas as they could would help them find the best solution.**

In other words, ideating really is just digging—unfiltered and automatic. It's letting your hands act before giving your mind enough time to develop a strategy for "smart digging." Just dig and you'll be surprised at what you find.

EXPERIMENTATION

After ideating, you should have a brimming list of good and bad, impossibly possible and possibly impossible ideas. The next part is testing them, evaluating results, and adjusting accordingly.

On one project, IDEO was tasked with designing a new dashboard feature for a luxury car. When experimenting with testing ideas, they filmed an existing car and used video effects to visualize potential features. The simplicity of the

---

68 Ibid.

prototyping led to the ability to cycle through ideas and get feedback on them rapidly.[69]

But experimenting isn't just about sharing prototypes for existing ideas and getting feedback to solve a problem for a client; experimenting for the sake of experimentation is equally important.

At my school, we have a secret design lab tucked away in the basement of our library. Nobody really knows about it, but they have an entire "Maker Hub," there, with Legos, clay, button-makers, and more. Sometimes, I just walk into the lab and grab a bunch of random items. I tinker with them somewhat randomly to create little houses and prototype product mockups.

Sometimes, when I walk in with the intention to simply experiment with whatever tools I have, I make something kind of cool. The other day, for example, I made an upside-down garage out of architecture tools (Bristol paper, Exacto knives, glue...etc.) for flying cars. Maybe Tesla or Google will need an upside-down garage designer in the future—who knows?

69 Kelley, Tom, and David Kelley. 2012 "Reclaim Your Creative Confidence". 2012. *Harvard Business Review*. Accessed November 8 2018. https://hbr.org/2012/12/reclaim-your-creative-confidence.

So, there are two predominant structures of experimentation.

1. Testing and prototyping an idea. This is digging when you know what you're looking for and not stopping until you find it.

2. Starting with tools and playing around until you maybe stumble on something great. This is accumulating the things you find while digging and then making something meaningful out if them.

As a whole, design thinking turns creativity into a formulaic process, one that is human-centric and low-risk. Design thinking is a type of play that increases creativity and learning exponentially.

Science and Design

At first look, design thinking can seem new and intimidating. As sad as it is, we aren't really trained to take a human-centric approach to problem solving, and we often don't find ourselves in nonjudgmental spaces where we're encouraged to brainstorm wild ideas. But the truth is, design thinking is simple. In fact, so simple that you likely learned a version of it in sixth grade biology.

We're all familiar with the scientific method in some sense. Most of us were introduced to it in a lab when we were asked to design and perform an experiment to test some kind of scientific hypothesis. The lab was the place where you could observe the effects of changing isolated variables, ask all the "what ifs?" you could think of, and collaborate with peers to iterate and reiterate the experiment. Within the lab, all of these principles were encouraged.

All we have to do is bring the lab environment outside the lab and into the larger world.

To me, design thinking is the scientific method removed from a lab and adopted as a lifestyle.

Introduction to the Method

I often think about my family history. My grandparents lived in the Lahore, the part of India that later became Pakistan. During the Partition of 1947, only my Nana (grandfather) and Pitaji (his father) happened to be around because the rest of the family had been vacationing in Mussouree (another part of India). When things began to escalate, Nana and Pitaji were forcibly removed from their home and left to fend for themselves. Millions of Hindus were fleeing Pakistan (just as many Muslims were fleeing India), so Nana and Pitaji headed toward the train station.

On their way, a Muslim elder driving a rickshaw and heading the opposite direction stopped them in their tracks. A complete stranger with nothing to gain or lose from helping them, he warned Nana and Pitaji that the train station was a trap where Hindus were being slaughtered mercilessly.

Pitaji and Nana had nothing except the clothes on their backs and whatever was left of their reputation when they joined their family in Mussouree. Their electrical agency in Lahore (now Pakistan) was very successful, so by the time the family relocated to Mumbai, people knew who they were. Someone from Philips spotted Pitaji on the street and immediately helped them get an agency in Mumbai.

Because two strangers made the decision to help, my grandparents were able to rebuild their lives, create a successful electric company from scratch, and raise their two daughters (one of whom is my mom) and one son.

Because of a spontaneous and serendipitous encounter made almost a century ago, I exist and have the life I have today. If my grandparents hadn't met that rickshaw driver, I don't know what would have happened.

Well, Edward Jenner is basically humanity's elderly Muslim rickshaw driver.

Edward Jenner, an English country doctor from Gloucestershire, is credited with making the first steps in eradicating smallpox from the world. When he was still a medical student, he noticed that milkmaids who had contracted cowpox, a disease that primarily affected cows, were naturally protected from smallpox. This disease caused severe skin eruptions and deathly fevers in humans. He then concluded that cowpox not only prevented smallpox but also could be transmitted from one person to another as a form of protection.[70]

So, to test his hypothesis, he used matter from blisters from someone with cowpox to infect James Phillips, his gardener's eight-year-old son. The boy then suffered typical symptoms of cowpox for nine days, and when he healed, Jenner promptly inoculated the boy with smallpox. The boy developed no symptoms, so Jenner concluded that he could not reject his hypothesis.[71]

The Latin word for cow is *vacca* and cowpox is *vaccinia*, so Jenner decided to call his newly created procedure *vaccination*. While many of his findings in his paper were initially

70 Riedel, Stefan. 2005. "Edward Jenner And The History Of Smallpox And Vaccination". *Proceedings (Baylor University. Medical Center)* 18 (1): 21. https://www.ncbi.nlm.nih.gov/pmc/articles/PMC1200696/.
71 Editors, History.com. 2018. "Jenner Tests Smallpox Vaccine". *HISTORY*. Accessed November 8 2018. https://www.history.com/this-day-in-history/jenner-tests-smallpox-vaccine.

rejected, Jenner distributed the inoculant to various surgeons and doctors who began administering it throughout England.[72]

To learn if he had created an appropriate cure, Jenner conducted a nationwide survey to see whether people who had cowpox were resistant to smallpox. The results confirmed his theory, and the use of the vaccination spread rapidly across England and not too long after, most European countries.[73]

Of course, scientists don't test vaccines on random children to determine their effectiveness. They have a system and steps that they test in a controlled setting. Labs are designated places to come up with hypotheses and test them using the established scientific method steps.

SCIENTIFIC METHOD STEPS

The scientific method, as most of us learn it, is broken down into the following steps:

1. Make an Observation
2. Ask a Question

72 Riedel, Stefan. 2005. "Edward Jenner And The History Of Smallpox And Vaccination". *Proceedings (Baylor University. Medical Center)* 18 (1): 21. https://www.ncbi.nlm.nih.gov/pmc/articles/PMC1200696/.
73 Ibid.

3. Form a hypothesis (testable explanation)
4. Make a prediction based on the hypothesis
5. Test the prediction
6. Iterate using the results to make new hypotheses or predictions

Let's quickly walk through an example because you learn the method by doing not reading.

1. Observe: I put bread in the toaster, and my bread does not toast.
2. Ask a question: Why won't my bread toast?
3. Formulate a hypothesis: Maybe the toaster is not plugged into the outlet.
4. Make a prediction: If I plug my toaster into the outlet, it will toast the bread.
5. Test the prediction: Check to see if the toaster is plugged in. If it is not plugged in, plug it in and see if bread toasts.
6. Iterate and Conclude: was my hypothesis correct? If the toast is toasting, then probably. If not, I go back to either step 3 or step 5 depending on where I went wrong. *Was it plugged into the outlet? Let's plug it into another outlet to see if that's the issue. If the bread toasts now, what is wrong with the first outlet? If the bread still doesn't toast, maybe there's something wrong with the toaster?*

The scientific method is an approach to analyzing the world around us, identifying problems, and generating solutions to those problems.[74] It delineates the process of discovery, which excites me more than anything else.

The only problem here is that learn the scientific method in school and keep it contained within the walls of the science labs.

Why? Because labs are spaces free of judgement, spaces specifically intended to house experimentation. Other places aren't as conducive to experimentation.

We have to make the scientific method mainstream. We have to bring the mindset and environment of a scientist and a lab, respectively, to the real world.

Outside the Lab

"The impulse to investigate can only be set free if you stop pretending to know answers that you don't," write authors and infamous "Freakonomics" economists Steven D. Levitt and Stephen J. Dubner in their book *Think Like a Freak.*[75]

---

74 "The Scientific Method". 2018. *Khan Academy.* Accessed November 8 2018. https://www.khanacademy.org/science/high-school-biology/hs-biology-foundations/hs-biology-and-the-scientific-method/a/the-science-of-biology.

75 Dubner, Stephen J, and Steven D Levitt. 2015. *Think Like A Freak.* HarperCollins USA.

One time, the two met with some executives from a large multinational retailer that was spending millions of dollars on TV commercials and print circulars in Sunday newspapers. They called in the "Steves" to consult on the relative effectiveness of these ads. The executives said they knew one thing: TV ads were four times more effective, dollar for dollar, than print ads.

The executives allegedly observed the effectiveness of the ads empirically and derived the aforementioned conclusion as a result: TV ads were more effective. Is this true? How did they know? The Steves tested this assumption by asking when these TV ads were running. They found that the ads only aired on Black Friday, Christmas, and Father's Day. "In other words, the company spent millions of dollars to entice people to go shopping precisely at the same time that millions of people were about to go shopping anyway."[76]

They could have very well had the same sales without spending a dime on TV commercials and instead relying on the general traffic increase caused by these holidays.

What about the print ads? How often did they run? When the authors asked these questions, they learned that the company had been buying newspaper ads for the past twenty years in

---

76 Ibid.

the same 250 US markets. "So how could they tell whether these ads were effective? They couldn't. With no variation whatsoever, it was impossible to know."[77]

The "Steves" wanted to determine the effectiveness of the ads.

"What if, we said, the company ran an experiment to find out? In science, the randomized control trial has been the gold standard of learning for hundreds of years, but why should scientists have all the fun?" In a randomized control trial, you divide your subjects into groups randomly. The randomness ensures that the groups remain as similar to each other as possible in all ways possible so you can test the effects of one variable on one group and compare it to the control group.

They described an experiment the company might run. In the experiment, they would select forty major markets across the country and randomly divide them into two groups. In the first group, the company would keep buying newspaper ads every Sunday. In the second group, they'd go totally dark—not a single ad. After three months, it would be easy to compare merchandise sales in the two groups to see how much the print ads mattered.

---

77 Ibid.

The executives were less than pleased, "Are you crazy? We can't possibly go dark in twenty markets; our CEO would kill us!"[78]

They then told a tale of a summer intern in Pittsburgh who once forgot to buy the ads in Pittsburgh, so the company didn't run any ads there. Embarrassed and ashamed, the intern profusely apologized for his flagrant oversight.

While the executives tried to change the subject to cover up their mistake, the Steves went back to check the data to see the effects of the infamous Pittsburgh pitfall.

The ad blackout hadn't affected the Pittsburgh sales at all.

"Now *that* we said, is valuable feedback. The company may be wasting hundreds of millions of dollars on advertising."

The executives would be able to know for sure how effective the ads were if they ran the forty-market experiment we mentioned earlier. When asked if they'd give it a shot, they said, "Are you crazy? We'd get fired."[79]

---

78 Ibid.
79 Ibid.

To this day, the company still runs newspaper ads, even though the only experiment they performed, albeit accidental, showed those ads don't work.

Why were these executives so allergic to experimentation?

One reason is that they aren't taught or trained to experiment. They usually make decisions based on a combination of precedent, instinct, and listening to superiors. Another is that they simply don't know how to design a good experiment. Most people hear "experiment" and think "science" and "lab."

The Steves, in this example, embrace the scientific method and use design thinking to bring experimentation outside the lab. Because of this, they are able to better consult businesses and identify points of improvement.

This story shows us that we can bring the lab wherever we go, and that the corporate and nonprofit worlds can clearly benefit from design thinking.

DESIGN AND BUSINESS

Quick and relevant aside here. The example above illustrates the information-action gap that traditional businesses experience between recognizing the importance of experimentation while also fearing making mistakes and failure. Students in school feel a similar conflict every day, because they're put at the center of this tug rope with performance on one side and innovation on the other.

I just want to make the case that Digging for Worms does substantially more good than harm.

McKinsey recently conducted what they believe to be the most extensive and comprehensive research into how design can unlock business value. In the study, they tracked design practices of three hundred publicly listed companies over a five-year period, collecting over two million pieces of financial data and recording over one hundred thousand design actions. The study found that design-led companies had 32 percent more revenue and 56 percent higher total returns to shareholders compared with other companies. This finding held true across three separate industries: medical technology, consumer goods, and retail banking.[80]

The study delineates four themes that increased revenue and total returns the most:

1. Analytical Leadership. Companies that track design's impact as any other important metric, like cost and revenue, saw

---

80 "The Business Value Of Design". 2018. *Mckinsey & Company*. Accessed November 8 2018. https://www.mckinsey.com/business-functions/ mckinsey-design/our-insights/the-business-value-of-design.

increased sales. McKinsey cites an example of how one gaming company that tracked a small usability tweak to its home page increased sales by 25 percent.

2. Cross-Functional Talent. Putting designers in a position to navigate freely between diverse teams makes user-centric design everyone's responsibility, and not a siloed function. McKinsey compares Spotify, a company that gives designers autonomy, to a packaged goods company that shoved designers behind PowerPoint to illustrate the power of cross-functional efforts.

3. Continuous Iteration. Encouraging research, prototyping, and iterating makes companies more successful. Just because the product launches does not mean iteration halts. One cruise company they analyzed constantly spoke with passengers, looked at data to determine which activities were consistently popular, and used machine learning to identify inefficiencies in the ship layout. They gather feedback and learn from it constantly to improve user experience over time.

4. User Experience. Companies that put users first and actually talk to them are more successful because they cater products to consumer needs. The simple act of writing out a consumer experience map goes a long way. McKinsey talks about a hotel that gives its visitors rubber ducks with the image of the city they're visiting to encourage them to collect more from the other hotel locations. Retention went up 3 percent.[81]

---

81 Ibid.

Clearly, when you bring design thinking principles into the business world, the results speak for themselves. Even though over 40 percent of the companies surveyed still don't talk to their end users during development and over 50 percent admit that they have "no objective way to assess or set targets for the output of their design teams," the potential of design-driven growth is exponential.[82]

With fast access to customers, it's easier than ever to develop empathy and put customers first. And, user-centric, analytically informed design is clearly worth the investment.

***

The scientific method is so simple, as simple as toast, in fact. It also feels doable because other people in the lab are doing it with you. And that's the challenge of bringing the scientific method out of the lab and into the real world, a problem IDEO embraces every day in its work.

---

82 Schwab, Katharine. 2018. "This Mckinsey Study Of 300 Companies Reveals What Every Business Needs To Know About Design For 2019". 2018. *Fast Company*. Accessed November 8 2018. https://www.fastcompany.com/90255363/this-mckinsey-study-of-300-companies-reveals-what-every-business-needs-to-know-about-design-for-2019?partner=rss&utm_source=facebook.com&utm_medium=social&utm_campaign=rss+fastcompany&utm_content=rss.

IDEO brings the scientific method out of the lab and into the open. Because they recognize the benefits of digging for worms, they are known as one of the most innovative and award-winning design firms in the world.

STEPS	SCIENTIFIC METHOD	IDEO	BOTTOM LINE
1	OBSERVE	FRAME A QUESTION	IDENTIFY WHAT'S INTERESTING ABOUT WHAT YOU'RE SEEING.
2	ASK A QUESTION	GATHER INSPIRATION	DO RESEARCH TO FIGURE OUT WHAT IS REALLY NEEDED.
3	HYPOTHESIZE	GENERATE IDEAS	THINK OF THINGS DIFFERENTLY AND PROPOSE SOLUTIONS.
4	PREDICT	MAKE IDEAS TANGIBLE	FIGURE OUT WHAT THE IDEAS LOOK LIKE IN REAL LIFE. #PROTOTYPE
5	TEST	TEST TO LEARN	EXPERIMENT FORWARD, GET FEEDBACK, AND BE WILLING TO LOOP BACK TO OTHER POINTS IN PROCESS.
6	ITERATE & CONCLUDE	SHARE THE STORY	SHARE THE IMPORTANCE OF YOUR DISCOVERY WITH OTHERS.

IDEO's design thinking steps mirror those of the scientific method shockingly (or perhaps not-so shockingly) well. IDEO creates a lab-like environment in which the scientific method, and its daughter, design thinking, flourish.

Digging for Worms is a call to take some inspiration from IDEO, and play with the mindset of a scientist and designer with you wherever you go. Doing so not only yields substantial tangible results in product and service design but also strengthens creativity and bolsters confidence.

CHAPTER 5

MONKEY BARS

Case 1:

You have $1,000, and you have two choices:

A: You have a 100 percent chance of gaining $500

B: You have a 50 percent chance of gaining $1,000 and a 50 percent of gaining $0

You have $2,000 and you have two more choices:

A: You have 100 percent chance of losing $500.

B: You have a 50 percent chance of losing $1,000 and a 50 percent chance of losing $0.

Logically, rational people can pick either A or B in both questions. However, the results of the study performed by behavioral finance founders Kahneman and Tversky showed that a significant majority of subjects chose A for question 1 and B for question 2.[83]

What is the motivation behind this decision?

Case 2:

You're walking back from work on a brisk summer evening. The sun has just started setting so Midtown Manhattan glows in the warm orange light. You glance up at the blue sky and down at the tourists populating Rockefeller Center, listening to soft tunes on your airpods.

Suddenly, your gaze locks. You see a man in a suit with sparkly eyes and a wide smile. Your feet melt into the concrete beneath you and your heart beats, you know, that kind of beat you're afraid the people around you can hear.

You stop in place, look away and look back. You can't just go up to him, right? You've never done that before, so you're scared.

---

83 Phung, Albert. "Behavioral Finance: Key Concepts – Prospect Theory". 2007. *Investopedia. Accessed November 8 2018.* https://www. investopedia.com/university/behavioral_finance/behavioral11.asp.

What's holding you back?

Case 3:

Blank page. The cursor click, click, clicks in front of you, staring you down. You have to write down the things you're thinking, but you don't even really know what you're thinking. You're certainly not thinking in any kind of particular order. You worked on the book so easily earlier this year, when publishing was so far away. Now, you're too scared to start.

One week, two weeks, three weeks go by and you haven't even opened the file to begin edits. November is coming. Is the book just going to write itself? Clearly, you know it won't. Rationally, you know you have to sit down, open your computer, and begin again. But every time you go to try, you choke.

The task seemed so large and impossible, so avoiding it altogether was all you thought you could do. Makes no sense really.

Three cases, all different variations of the same thing. What holds us back from taking that first leap? How do we get past that?

***

Monkey Bars: Turning Ambition into Action. Taking risks. Closing the gap between aspiration and action helps you achieve your full potential.

Suspended in the air, you extend your arm out and touch the next bar to make sure you can reach it. Feet dangling below and fingers white from gripping so hard above, you take a deep breath. You can't last much longer on that bar before your body gets so frustrated it collapses.

One, two, three, launch your body forward, the momentum pulling your hands to the next bar. Slow at first, but now you've got the rhythm.

Monkey bars is about figuring out what you want and not fearing the leap. It's the kind of play that scares you, until you try it.

***

Different things keep different people clutching to the bar for longer than others. In this chapter, we'll go over three common cases and propose solutions to combat each of them. Adopting the mindset of a risk-taker allows you to reach out and take that first leap so you can take another, and another, and another, and end up where you want to be.

CASE 1: FEAR OF THE UNKNOWN.

Ambition: Make the right choice.

Holdback: Focus on loss of stability.

Necessary Action: Focus on net gain.

I type on my computer, excited that the woman who sat next to me got off at Baltimore so I could sit criss-cross on the train. Enter handsome stranger, and with a flash of dimples I find myself nodding before he could even say, "This seat taken?" with that tinted charm you just know gets him unreasonably long extensions on papers.

It's spring break, but he's in a suit, so I'm curious. He's a junior in business school, on his way to his "Placement Day" to figure out which department at Credit Suisse he'll intern at over the summer. I start talking to him, fully expecting him to be that obnoxious Wall Street guy with a skinny tie and apple watch who still brags about his SAT scores. I know, *probably* an unfair judgement. In this case, I could not have been more wrong.

We sat behind two five-year-old boys singing *Wake Me Up Before You Go-Go* (how did these kids know that song?) and arguing over whether to play war or color and in front of an older man talking about his years in prison and giving advice to a young girl heading out for spring break. Fittingly, as two twenty-year-olds, clinging on to adolescence while approaching the precipice of true adulthood, our conversation demonstrated that tension between youthful creativity and increased responsibility, between performance and innovation culture.

"I hate the business school."

Elaborate.

"The culture is so unhealthy. The classes are graded on a curve, so it's rare to find people who believe that helping others doesn't hurt themselves. For me, I know I'm not in that 10 percent who gets an A, so if I can help someone else, I will. But I guess that's also why people are surprised that I got this internship."

How did he get it then?

"I just talked to people more genuinely than others. I take sociology classes so that I don't get corrupted by the business school culture. I don't know... there are smarter people than me for sure. But I think personality matters a lot. I stopped trying to be busy for the sake of being busy. I just wanted to relax and focus on things I cared about in college, and the moment I made that choice, I started to become a better person all around."

Boom. Revolutionary. I always thought everyone who sought these kinds of internships were just blindly chasing prestige, but not all of them are. Train guy, for example, doesn't even know that he wants to do IB with his life. Instead, he's using it as an opportunity to live in a fun city for the summer and learn new things. Good for him, I thought.

He told me about his brothers and their dreams and goals, his passion for tutoring children, and how he would have majored in sociology and government if he could go back. Wow. Here's a person who values himself beyond metrics and sees beyond the myopic pressure to "sound impressive" in business school.

Train guy is an exception to the average pipeline student. I want to be clear and say that I understand the appeal of the masses, and this is not meant to criticize anyone who truly aspires to work and be successful in the more popular fields. But many people don't; instead, they subscribe to a cycle of chasing the next most prestigious thing because it feels safe and reliable.

In his book, *Smart People Should Build Things*, Andrew Yang, founder of Venture for America, explains why these loop-trap mechanisms work:

Unfortunately, hardworking, academically gifted young people are kind of lazy when it comes to determining direction. If you give them a hoop to jump through, jumping through that hoop can take two, twenty, or two hundred hours, and it won't make a big difference. But they are quite lazy when it comes to figuring out what path to take or—more profoundly— building their own path. They're trained to get the grade or ace the application. That is what has made them successful in most every conventional respect each step of the way up to their senior year in college, at the point that this process is well under way.[84]

He even goes so far as to equate us to circus animals, incentivized by treats given by some aloof beneficiary holding up hoops for us to jump through. Once we realize other things exist, once we look beyond the shiny brochures and sleek blue blazers, we give ourselves options.[85]

But we have been trained, through our education system, to value performance and prestige over risk and innovation.

---

84 Yang, Andrew. 2014. *Smart People Should Build Things.*
85 Ibid.

Ken Robinson, education disruptor and speaker of the most-watched Ted Talk *How Schools Kill Creativity*, articulates the flaws of the system beautifully in the following quote:

Public schools were not only created in the interests of industrialism—they were created in the image of industrialism. In many ways, they reflect the factory culture they were designed to support. This is especially true in high schools, where school systems base education on the principles of the assembly line and the efficient division of labor. Schools divide the curriculum into specialist segments: some teachers install math in the students, and others install history. They arrange the day into standard units of time, marked out by the ringing of bells, much like a factory announcing the beginning of the workday and the end of breaks. Students are educated in batches, according to age, as if the most important thing they have in common is their date of manufacture. They are given standardized tests at set points and compared with each other before being sent out onto the market. I realize this isn't an exact analogy and that it ignores many of the subtleties of the system, but it is close enough.[86]

The factory system outputs freshly minted replica models and companies perform calculations to buy in bulk. It's easy to go through the factory system, because the steps are so obvious:

---

86 Robinson, Ken, and Lou Aronica. 2014. *The Element*. New York: Penguin Books.

prepare for cases, edit resumes, network within companies.. etc. Anyone can learn them to achieve their end goal.

The factory model is great for those who know why they want to do what they want to do, but sometimes, the factory starts the assembly line so quickly that people don't even get the chance to think.

It's predictable. We're scared to take a risk because we're scared to lose control of the predictability. How do we overcome this?

PROSPECT THEORY

Kahneman and Tversky explain the results to the questions in Case 1 by introducing prospect theory—the idea that people tend to value gains and losses differently from one another, and, as a result, will base decisions on perceived gains rather than perceived losses.[87] In other words, we feel a more profound feeling when we lose something than when we gain something of equivalent value.

Consider the following illustration. How would you react to the following two situations:

---

87 Phung, Albert. "Behavioral Finance: Key Concepts – Prospect Theory". 2007. *Investopedia. Accessed November 8 2018.* https://www. investopedia.com/university/behavioral_finance/behavioral11.asp.

1. You find $75 on the ground
2. You lose $75 then subsequently find $150 on the ground

If you felt a more positive reaction to the first situation, you're experiencing prospect theory bias. Kahneman goes further to prove that the amount of pain experienced by loss of money outweighs the amount of joy gained from finding money, resulting in a net "loss" of utility.

Thankfully, he also proposes a potential solution to countering prospect theory—hedonic framing.

Hedonic framing suggests that you should think about losses and gains in the following ways:

- If you have the choice to think of something as one huge gain or a number of smaller gains, think of it as a bunch of smaller gains. This maximizes the positive feelings.
- If you have to the choice to think of something as one huge loss or a number of smaller losses, think of it as one huge loss. This minimizes negative feelings by ripping off the Band-Aid instead of peeling it off slowly.
- When you have a combination of gain and loss, as in our example of losing $75 and then finding $150, it's best to think about the smaller net gain.[88]

---

88 Ibid.

So, there is a way to grab the next monkey bar. You're clenching the first bar because you're focused on what you will lose—stability, predictability, comfort—when you let go of the first bar. Instead, **you can focus on what you'll gain by taking the leap.** More often than not, it's a net gain.

CASE 2: FEAR OF FEARS YOU'VE ALWAYS HAD.

Ambition: Do something bold that puts you out there.

Current action: Do nothing at all.

Necessary Action: Make your fears second nature by shifting focus.

Albert Bandura was a psychologist who worked to understand how behavioral modeling could help people overcome phobias. One specific experiment worked with participants who all had snake phobia. He created a methodology that cured people of their phobias by gradual and systematic desensitization.[89]

He would invite the test subject into a room and guide them through a series of steps. He would start by telling the subject

---

89 Bandura, Albert. 1977. "Self-Efficacy: Toward A Unifying Theory Of Behavioral Change.". *Psychological Review* 84 (2): 191–215. doi:10.1037//0033-295x.84.2.191.

that there was a snake in the room next door and that they were going to go in there. Participants rejected the idea immediately.

Albert used a combination of relaxation techniques—to assuage anxiety—and small steps until the patient was in the room with the snake—to eliminate denial and foster acceptance in the mind of the participant. Eventually, the participant would touch the snake and effectively cure their phobia.[90]

What does this have to do with asking a stranger out?

You guessed it! Boys are snakes. You're scared at first but eventually become neutral toward them.

Ha-ha just kidding.

Lots of people have phobias, like firemen who won't fight grass fires and plumbers who only work indoors and biologists who are scared of dirt. The bottom line here is that there is a way, referred to by Albert as "guided mastery" to overcome phobias.[91]

---

90 Ibid.
91 Kelley, Tom, and David Kelley. 2012 "Reclaim Your Creative Confidence". 2012. *Harvard Business Review*. Accessed November 8 2018. https://hbr.org/2012/12/reclaim-your-creative-confidence.

Such a process, he concludes, not only allows you to overcome your fear, but also contributes to greater self-efficacy in other aspects of life. Prior to desensitization treatment, Bandura measured their self-efficacy and performance expectations and found they were quite low. He concluded, however, that the desensitization treatment increased the strength of the subjects' perceived self-efficacy.

Eliminating a fear requires perceiving that you can eliminate it. How do you put yourself through an informal "guided mastery" process to eliminate a fear and increase self-efficacy?

PREVENTION VS. PROMOTION

Disclaimer: I don't typically advocate for typecasting, as I believe people are malleable and constantly growing, changing, and improving. The following grouping is *not* intended to suggest that you figure out what group you fit in and remain in that box. Instead, it's intended to help you better understand what could motivate you better to address a fear.

Heidi Grant, Harvard PhD and social psychologist, has dedicated much of her research to the science of motivation. She suggests that there are two primary motivational foci—promotion-focused and prevention-focused.[92]

---

92 Grant, Heidi. 2013. "Do You Play To Win—Or To Not Lose?". 2013. *Harvard Business Review. Accessed November 8 2018. https://hbr.*

In short, promotion-focused people tend to see their goals as "creating a path to gain...and concentrate on the rewards that will accrue when they achieve them."

On the other hand, "prevention-focused people tend to see their goals as "responsibilities...and concentrate on staying safe."[93]

Some more typical characteristics are summarized in the table below.

	PROMOTION	PREVENTION
PROS	- WORK QUICKLY - CONSIDER ALTERNATIVES - OPEN TO NEW OPPORTUNITIES - OPTIMISTIC - PLAN FOR BEST CASE SCENARIO - SEEK POSITIVE FEEDBACK	- WORK DELIBERATELY - PREPARED FOR THE WORST - USE TRIED AND RELIABLE METHODS - CRITICAL - PREFER STABILITY
CONS	- PRONE TO ERROR - IMPULSIVE - UNPREPARED - DEJECTED WHEN THINGS GO WRONG - LOSE STEAM WITHOUT POSITIVE FEEDBACK	- STRESSED BY SHORT DEADLINES - UNCOMFORTABLE WITH PRAISE - WORRIED OR ANXIOUS WHEN THINGS GO WRONG - RISK AVERSE

org/2013/03/do-you-play-to-win-or-to-not-lose.
93 Ibid.

According to Heidi, most people have a dominant type, and most people upon exposure to this framework immediately know which type that is[94]. It can be beneficial to know what your tendencies are so you can recognize patterns in what you pay attention to, what you value, and what you feel when you fail.

But while each of us tends to favor one over the other, we all use both perspectives regularly. Each of our goals requires a personalized approach to tackling them. Heidi talks about how some goals are "be good" goals and some goals are "get better" goals.[95]

Once we figure out what *kind* of goals we're setting, we can figure out which focus—prevention or promotion—will help address it.

FRAMING THE GOAL

How do you feel when you hear:

"You are going to shoot five penalties. Your aspiration is to score at least three times."

vs.

---

94 Ibid.
95 Ibid.

"You are going to shoot five penalties. Your obligation is to not miss more than twice."

German researchers gave semi-professional soccer coaches the direction to hype their players with one of those two statements, one slightly more promotional (play to win) and the other slightly more preventative (play not to lose).[96]

You probably wouldn't expect a slight difference in wording to affect these highly trained, motivated, and practiced players. But, of course, it had a huge impact.

Players who received instruction that fit with their dominant motivational focus did significantly better than those with a mismatch. Specifically, prevention-dominant players scored nearly twice as often when they received statement two.[97]

How does this apply to tackling a fear that we've had forever?

We have to identify what kind of goal we have. Heidi helps us out.

"Promotion-focused goals are thought about in terms of achievement and accomplishment. They are about doing

---

96 Ibid.
97 Ibid.

something you would ideally like to do… they are about maximizing gains (and avoiding missed opportunities).

"Prevention-focused goals are thought about in terms of safety and danger. They are about fulfilling responsibilities, doing the things you feel you *ought* to do…they are about minimizing *losses*, trying to hang on to what you've got."[98]

The key here is you can choose how to view your goal and what approach to take when addressing it. You can rebrand a promotional goal as a preventative one, and vice versa, using *words*.

USE YOUR WORDS

Our words, specifically the ones we say to ourselves, have immense power in creating an intentional visualization that affects how we perceive reality, and, by extension, what happens to us. I learned this concept as the Power of the Spoken Word, but there are several names for it.

Here's an example my dad always shares to illustrate.

What do you visualize when you see the following pair of statements?

---

98 Ibid.

"Don't slam the door!"

vs.

"Shut the door gently."

Take a second to think about what image popped into your head as you read each statement.

For most people, the first evokes a dynamic snapshot of a door slamming angrily. The second, on the other hand, pictures a variation of someone gingerly closing a door.

What's stopping me from asking this guy out?

How I felt:

Preventative: *I'm fine without him. I've never done this so I have no idea what the best way to approach this is. I'd like to avoid embarrassment and disappointment.*

I walked back and forth a couple times, changing my decision with every step. I went around the block twice and even began jogging away.

What I said to myself:

Promotion: *What's there to lose? Who cares if he rejects you. You don't even know him. You want to be bold and confident? Then do it. You'll only miss out by not taking chances.*

I walk up to the waitress serving his table, tiptoeing inconspicuously so as to not display my internal argument with my rationality.

"Hi. I have a really weird favor to ask," I blurt before I think. My voice sounds even despite my trembling fingers.

She smiles, skeptical but interested. "What is it?"

I fidget a little, tap dancing back and forth, awkward but eager. "Can you give that guy my number? That one in the white over there."

I write a note. I tell her to hand him the note when I leave and to tell him I was cute. After a bit of chitchat, I sprint away to central park and leave the rest to destiny.

I turned a preventative fear into a promotional goal with the words I was saying to myself. That's how I overcame a fear I've always had. And let me tell you, that was the fastest and most enjoyable run I've ever had.

CASE 3: OVERWHELMED BY ASPIRATION.

Ambition: Do Something Unbelievably Great.

Current Action: Don't start so you don't mess it up.

Necessary Action: Break it down into small steps.

Sir Isaac Newton was the single most influential scientist of the seventeenth century. Most people know that he was the first to discover that white light was a spectrum of colors, the first to develop an understanding of the basic physical principle of gravity, and the first to work on the beginnings of calculus. There is no doubt that Isaac Newton, with his wide range of discoveries, changed our understanding of the world around us irreversibly.

But what turned out to eventually become a huge feat started out with small steps. Newton wasn't as much a big thinker as he was a simple observer.

When Newton was at Cambridge in the late seventeenth century, he dove into the study of gravitational force. His research was published in 1687 and was titled *Principia*. In *Principia*, Newton breaks down the workings of the solar system into "simple" equations. He described how the moon orbits the Earth, a realization that began as a simple observation and spiraled into a monumental assertion.[99]

As Newton eloquently puts it, "To explain all nature is too difficult a task for any one man or even any one age. Tis much better to do a little with certainty and leave the rest for others that come after than to explain all things by conjecture without making sure of any thing."[100]

In other words, when you have high ambitions and dreams in the clouds, start by taking small steps.

SMALL STEPS

When the authors of *Think Like a Freak* are asked to consult businesses, governments or researchers, they think small:

"Every big problem has been thought about endlessly by people much smarter than we are. The fact that it remains a problem means it is too damned hard to be cracked in full… Sure, there are some truly brilliant people out there and they

---

99 Whipps, Heather. Science, Live. 2008. "How Isaac Newton Changed The World". *Live Science*. Accessed November 8 2018. https://www.livescience.com/4965-isaac-newton-changed-world.html.

100 Bariso, Justin. 2018. "12 Brilliant Quotes From The Genius Mind Of Sir Isaac Newton". 2016. *Inc.Com*. Accessed November 8 2018. https://www.inc.com/justin-bariso/12-brilliant-quotes-from-the-genius-mind-of-sir-isaac-newton.html.

probably *should* think big. For the rest of us, thinking big means you'll spend a lot of time tilting at windmills."[101]

They then bring up the example of education reform. Trillions of dollars have been spent on larger education reform efforts, on a top-down disruptive initiative. But in these attempts to attack a grand problem, students themselves become overlooked.

"Might there be some small, simple, cheap, intervention that could help millions of students?"

Three economists, Paul Glewwe, Albert Park, and Meng Zhao, solved big problems by thinking small. They found that one in four children has poor eyesight and that 60 percent of "problem learners" have subpar eyesight.

In Gansu, a remote province in China, the economists found that only fifty-nine of the twenty-five hundred students who needed eyeglasses had them. So, they distributed free glasses to half of the students and observed the results. After a year, the "newly bespectacled" students learned 25 to 50 percent more than their peers.[102]

---

101 Dubner, Stephen J, and Steven D Levitt. 2015. *Think Like A Freak.* HarperCollins USA.
102 Ibid.

The economists of course cared about the bigger picture issue of access to education and systems of education, but their decision to focus small led them to generating a solution that made a people-level impact.

Whether it's working with a team to tackle a problem like education or working individually to move towards a big goal, starting with small steps is the way to begin.

Consider the following example:

"I want to be prime minister."

Manu Goswami, more lovingly known as "Swish," a twenty-year old TEDx speaker, venture capitalist, UN Youth Ambassador, and serial entrepreneur, told me about how he turns ambition into action.

"A lot of people would write that down as the number one plan, but I break it down into one, three, and five-year goals."

Aha. Big goal, small steps.

A one-year goal might be buy political membership into a party. A three-year plan could be volunteer for three political campaigns. And a five-year plan could be to start *thinking* about running for a local position. So, planning short-term goals is important, but over-planning is counterproductive.

He told me some of the things he thinks about when turning a big ambition into action.

Planning is important, but planning too much leads to over-thinking and paralysis. He says that planning is important but many people plan the long term immediately while neglecting the short term.

"Ninety percent of people don't turn ambition into action because they spend too much time planning." A lot people go through months thinking about an idea and then they "jinx themselves out of it to the point where they start thinking about holes."

Here we arrive at our next way to approach a problem that seems too big to handle.

GIVE YOURSELF AN IMPOSSIBLE DEADLINE

As we know from Newton's laws of physics, "every object persists in its state of rest or uniform motion in a straight line unless it is compelled to change that state by the forces impressed on it."

In other words, you will stay where you are doing what you are doing unless a force acts upon you to change that.

Sometimes, putting yourself under immense time constraints forces you to move before you have time to stress about moving. In a way, it eclipses old stress by focusing on an overwhelming quantity of new stress, forcing you to move forward instead of cling to what you have. You do much more than you think you can do.

John Keefe, senior editor at radio station WNYC, did exactly that after a colleague complained that her mom had to wait at bus stops never knowing when the next bus would come.

This kind of problem would take months to solve if planned and executed through a structured organization like the New York City Transit.

As told by Tom Kelley, partner at IDEO, in an HBS article,

John, who does not work for the transit authority, said "Give me till the end of the day." He bought an 800 number, figured out how to access real-time bus data, and linked it to text-to-speech technology. Within twenty-four hours, he had set up a service that allowed bus riders to call in, input their bus stop number, and hear the location of the approaching bus. John applies the same fearless attitude to his work at WNYC.[103]

I'm not sure if John knew if he could pull of what he did in the time that he did, but either way, he definitely stretched his limits. Now, he's a little less scared of big ambitions.

An impossible deadline is daunting, but it forces you to get moving.

During my first year of college, I was selected for a GU Impacts, a prestigious fellowship program. The program places us at various social enterprises across the globe to work as interns of all trades, but it only paid for interns with certain academic majors, because of the specificity of the grants. It seems I did not fit the bill, so I had to pay the bill.

I decided there must be another way, so I quickly found a research grant I could apply for.

The Kalorama Research Grant is awarded to students who propose a thorough humanities-centric research proposal within the designated time frame. A faculty mentor must write a recommendation letter confirming soundness of the proposal and

---

103 Kelley, Tom, and David Kelley. 2012 "Reclaim Your Creative Confidence". 2012. *Harvard Business Review.* Accessed November 8 2018. https://hbr.org/2012/12/reclaim-your-creative-confidence.

willingness to be an ongoing advisor for the duration of the project.

It then proceeded to list requirements of the proposal, average page length (20 pages), and sample proposals.

Okay... I can do this. I just have to think of something I'd want to research.

I scrolled to the bottom of the page.

Deadline: Tomorrow.

It was about 8pm, and I had an econ midterm at 9am the next morning. I scrapped the midterm—I was determined to get this money.

I plugged my headphones in and began piecing together a random research proposal on the fly—something related to my internship but not too related so that I could do both at the same time. I knew no faculty in the humanities who would pass as an advisor, so as soon as I had a draft of the proposal, I cold-emailed 15 professors in desperation at midnight.

Long story short, within 24 hours, I wrote a 20-page research proposal, met an entirely new faculty member and convinced her to write me a recommendation letter, and received the grant.

The extreme timeline forced me to do a lot in a short amount of time. It helped me realize that I shouldn't be scared of a big ambition; instead, I should just stretch a little further and see if I can grab it.

***

Monkey bars is about taking risks and overcoming fears. When you swing from bar to bar, each time you move forward you let go of something comfortable. For a moment, you dangle freely in the air until you grab the next one.

It's really fun to see what you can do when you let go of what's holding you back.

CHAPTER 6

TAG

———

So annoying, and yet so catchy, toeing that all-too-familiar love-hate line ever so gently, simultaneously making your blood simmer and your heart sing...everyone knows the song...

♫ *it's a small world after all...it's a small world after all... it's a small world after all, it's a small, small, world.* ♫

And, repeat, repeat, repeat, until the tune burns into your brain and rattles in your head for pretty much eternity.

While the Magic Kingdom ride's cons might outweigh its pros, the sentiment it shares is quite sweet. It takes the rider on a tour of the world through dancing dolls, showcasing different cultures and regions through costumes and settings.

All the dolls dance together to the song—a nice illustration of human fraternity and, more specifically, the small-world phenomenon.

The first significant study of the small-world phenomenon occurred in the 1960s, when social psychologist Stanley Milgram asked randomly chosen "starter" individuals to each try forwarding a letter to a designated "target" person in suburban Massachusetts. The participants had the target's name, address, occupation, and some personal information. The only caveat was that they were not allowed to mail the letter directly to the target.[104]

Instead, they could only advance the letter by forwarding it to a single acquaintance, who then could continue the chain and forward to another acquaintance, to another, and so on. The objective was to reach the target as soon as possible.

About a third of the letters arrived at the target, in a median of six steps. This experiment served as the inspiration for things like that viral game, "Six Degrees of Kevin Bacon," which tried to show that you can pick any famous person and connect them to Kevin Bacon in six or less steps. More importantly, Milgram's experiment taught us two things about large social networks:

---

104 Easley, David, and Jon Kleinberg. 2018. *Networks, Crowds, And Markets*. Johanneshov: MTM.

- Short paths exist in abundance
- People don't need a "map" of their network in order to find short paths[105]

These are powerful conclusions. Recognizing that you can reach almost anyone through acquaintances, or weak ties, shows the power of our interconnectedness today.

Mark Granovetter, in his PhD research, illustrates further just how important weak ties can be. He interviewed people who had recently changed employers to learn about how they discovered their new jobs. Through this, he found that most people had learned about their current job through personal contacts they described as "acquaintances."[106]

We'll get into some more network theory later in the chapter, but the bottom line is that people are connected, and there is so much potential in the people who surround us to teach us, challenge us, and expose us to new opportunities.

***

Tag: sometimes we need other people to believe in us, inform us, and challenge us.

———

105 Easley, David, and Jon Kleinberg. 2018. *Networks, Crowds, And Markets*. Johanneshov: MTM.
106 Ibid.

When you play tag, you play with a group of other kids. Some you know, and some you don't. You run around either tagging or avoiding being tagged, and you interact with others in the spirit of the game.

Someone you know or don't might tag you, passing you the baton to chase purposefully instead of flee frantically.

Tag is all about playing with people and relationships. You play by taking that first step in asking to join an existing game. Others help you play, perhaps teaching you new variations of it you had never learned before. And you play to make friends and broaden your personal sphere.

**

NETWORK THEORY BACKGROUND

Network Science uses graph theory to model interconnectedness. It's a robust field of study that permeates virtually every other field, from terrorism prevention to cascading customer influence, and seeks to simplify our increasingly networked world through data and visualization.

Networks are often mapped using graph theory. Graphs at a base level, are comprised of two components: nodes (represent people, groups, actors, etc.), and edges (connect nodes based on defined relationships). Strong ties, which refer to close and frequent social contacts, tend to be in tightly liked areas of the graph, whereas weak ties, which are more casual and distinct social contacts, tend to cross between those regions.[107]

In this way, we can see social networks as dense clumps of strong ties interacting with each other through weaker ties. When we apply this framework to the real world, we can identify structural holes between parts of the network that interact very little with each other. On a global scale, we can see how weak ties can link together distant parts of the world, as we've seen with the small-world phenomenon.

One of the most fundamental notions about social network analysis is homophily—the principle that we tend to be similar to our friends. While we certainly have friends who are different than us, viewed collectively, our friends are generally similar to us in age, ethnicity, affluence, beliefs, opinions, etc. In aggregate, we are connected to people who are similar to us.[108]

This is nothing new. Platitudes like "birds of a feather flock together," and quotes from Plato, "similarity begets

---

107 Ibid.
108 Ibid.

friendship," and Aristotle, "[people] love those who are like themselves," confirm the presence of homophily.

That's where weak ties come in. Take a look at the image below from <u>Networks, Crowds, and Markets:</u>

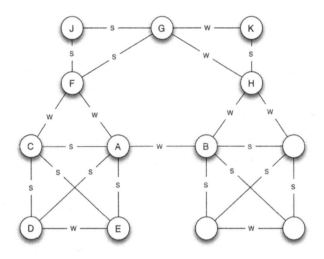

The "W" stands for weak, and "S" for strong.[109]

Let's say that the left side, A-F exhibits homophily and the right side also exhibits homophily. Then the weak tie linking A and B becomes especially important because it makes it more likely that the groups will mix and get exposed to new things.

---

109 Image source: Easley, David, and Jon Kleinberg. 2018. *Networks, Crowds, And Markets.* Johanneshov: MTM.

Let's say, for example, that D really wants a job working at the company B works at. Because D is linked to A, D is more likely to meet B and form a relationship with B. A, knowing what A knows, may also be able to connect D to B intentionally. If the weak tie between A and B did not exist, it would be much more difficult for D to meet B.

Okay, why am I telling you this?

Tag is all about playing with the people around you. To do that effectively, you should know how you are connected to those around you and how the people around you can help. You should know how powerful it can be to capitalize on your weak ties.

There are so many ways to play tag, and we'll go over three interpretations of the principle in this chapter.

WHEN YOUR WEAK TIES TAG YOU

When Rome was rapidly developing and builders scoured every inch of land looking to construct, one building society embarked on an overambitious project. After constructing the walls for five houses, each six stories high, the company went bankrupt and left the project incomplete. All that remained was an abandoned skeleton composed of walls and holes.

This abandoned building became a home for beggars, a refuge for criminals, and a breeding ground for infection. As thousands of people flocked into its collapsing walls, the "Quartiere di San Lorenzo" became notorious as the "shame of Italy." Neither the police nor the government dared to go close enough to help. Soon, a wealthy building group offered an olive branch and refurnished one of the buildings so that it could more comfortably house one thousand people.[110] Problem not solved, but baby steps for sure.

But while the parents left during the day, their wild and uncivilized kids were free to act on their every whim, posing a threat and damaging the houses. The director of the compound decided to confine all the children in a sort of prison to keep them out of trouble. People knew this was a temporary solution, but no one had the guts to do anything about it. That is, until they asked Maria Montessori for advice.

As the first female physician in Italy equipped with expertise in hygiene, she demanded changes to food and sanitation. While these were necessary, Dr. Montessori recognized they were not enough. The society ladies and bankers pouring money into improving the housing situation had

---

110 "The First Casa Dei Bambini | Montessori Australia Foundation". 2018. *Montessori.Org.Au.* Accessed November 8 2018. https://montessori.org.au/first-casa-dei-bambini.

little interest in the children themselves. With no toys, no school, no teacher, and no guidance, the children had been forgotten.[111]

Maria wanted to change that.

"It was striking at the time this interest of society imbued with the idea that their giving hygienic houses to the homeless would be the means of purifying the evil core in their midst."[112]

Maria didn't understand why nobody had taken the children into consideration. Why were they all dressed in the same heave blue drill? Why weren't they allowed to move their arms freely? Why were they all crying miserably? How can they be better, more literate and less high-risk than their parents if they aren't exposed to more?[113]

So she brought in some toys from her work in experimental psychology. She gave the children the toys and stepped back, deciding to focus on observing instead of interfering. Left all alone, the children began to work with concentration

111 Ibid.
112 Ibid.
113 "Maria Montessori Biography And History | American Montessori Society ". 2018. Amshq.Org. Accessed November 8 2018. https:// amshq.org/Montessori-Education/History-of-Montessori-Education/ Biography-of-Maria-Montessori.

and transform. From timid and wild to sociable and communicative, their personalities grew and they "flourished in health as if they had been secretly fed on some nourishing food—and so they had, but in their spirit." They brought consideration and gratitude back to their families, who noticed the change and subsequently asked Maria to teach them to read.[114]

"I gave them the alphabet... I analyzed the words for them and showed that each sound of the words had a symbol by which it could be materialized." That's it. She just gave them the tool and let them run with it.

"The whole world became interested in this phenomenal activity of writing of these children who were so young and whom nobody taught. These children worked all the time without being forced by anyone to do so." Their fame spread so quickly that soon after the news spread, even the Queen of Italy made a trip to Italy's once most shameful corner to meet the children she'd heart about.[115]

Not only did Maria Montessori exhibit astute understanding of design thinking and scientific method principles, as

114 "The First Casa Dei Bambini | Montessori Australia Foundation". 2018. *Montessori.Org.Au.* Accessed November 8 2018. https://montessori.org.au/first-casa-dei-bambini.
115 Ibid.

we talked about in Chapter 4, she also happened to change millions of people's lives for centuries to come.

She was a weak tie to all those students. In fact, whoever asked her to consult on the hygiene was a weak tie to Maria herself. Even though nobody asked her for help beyond her specialization, she impacted all of those kids and changed the landscape of education permanently.

Maria was tagged by a weak tie to become another weak tie to the kids she didn't know. The person who asked Maria to consult the project helped Maria play in the whole new challenging sphere of education; he helped connect her to her destiny. And Maria gave hope to hundreds of children who believed in nothing and who nobody believed in. **Her weak-tie relationship equipped her with a fresh perspective to tackle problems the strong ties were too close to see.**

WHEN YOUR STRONG TIES TAG YOU

I opened *Azulejo*, our next assignment for Spanish Literature, and stared blankly at a fifteenth century poem written by some old famous guy who I cared little about and a lot to ignore. What did this stuff mean? How was this going to be useful in my life? I read the poem in English and Spanish and English and Spanish, googling analyses and watching

PowerPoints. I spent weeks alone trying to give this poem a chance, trying to find *something* interesting.

Near the end of the first term, I went to my Spanish Lit class, pink slip in hand, ready to ride this freedom ticket far, far away from Juan Manuel and Pablo Neruda and Borges and everyone else whose words found their destiny in my textbook. My friends encouraged me to drop the class, saying things like "it's a hard class," "you're so busy!" and even, "it's the mature thing to do."

The pink slip peaked out of my folder, just enough to catch Señora's eye.

"You're not dropping this class."

Shocked, I didn't even respond. I stayed in the class because I had no choice. I had tears in my eyes that day, but Señora didn't flinch. She somehow knew how things would turn out.

Surprise, surprise, I fell in love with Spanish Literature. After that day, we shifted to more modern texts, ones that I could relate to. I remember reading *La Casa de Bernarda Alba*, a play about a family of six daughters and a bossy mother (an allegory of sorts of Spain under dictator Francisco Franco), and spending hours analyzing the interpersonal relations between characters. I loved finding literary devices, writing essays comparing stories, and understanding the impact a given story had in its time period.

I didn't expect to like Spanish Literature, but I did. I just needed a little push.

This is the most obvious way to play tag—letting the people you know tag you. Everyone has a story like this; nearly any story about mentorship or how one individual inspired another involves a strong tie moment.

One of my favorite examples of a strong mentor is Pete Carroll, coach of the Seattle Seahawks and former coach of other NFL and some college teams. His coaching style implements a healthy dose of fun and capitalizes on the uniqueness of each individual in his team. He had themes for each day of the week – Tell the Truth Monday, Competition Wednesday, Turnover Thursday. He blared music throughout practice to keep energy high but also challenge his players to focus around distraction.

"It basically comes down to taking care of the people in your program and making them the best they can be – not giving up on them and never failing to be there for them."[116]

---

116 Trotter, Jim. 2014. "The power of positive coaching." Accessed November 8 2018. https://www.si.com/2014/01/23/pete-carroll-seattle-seahawks-super-bowl-48.

In his four years, Carroll has taken the Seahawks from 5–11 the year before he arrived to 7–9, 7–9, 11–5, and 13–3.

Carroll improves the lives of everyone around him, even beyond his players. He founded non-profit organizations focused on tackling gang violence by empowering former gang members with education and training. He speaks directly to gang members, encouraging them to overcome their circumstance, often offering his personal cell number to foster an authentic relationship.[117]

Figures who are already in mentorship or authoritative roles have a strong tie relationship centered around helping. They're already close to you, so they know you and should want to help.

This is the most passive way to play tag. This is the kid who stands out in the open waiting to be tagged by his buddy.

Seems simple enough. The danger here, however, is that those who are closest to you, while they have potential to help you greatly, also can tackle you and leave you face-down in the mud.

---

117 "Pete Carroll In 60 Minutes". 2008. *Vimeo*. Accessed November 8 2018. https://vimeo.com/2529346.

So it's no longer about how you play tag but instead *who you play tag with.* Who do you intentionally keep close and why? Whose advice to you listen to and why? Is it helpful, hurtful, or neutral? Do these people play fair or conspire to get a head start?

WHO TO PLAY TAG WITH

Exhaust fogs the windows and heat builds up inside the car. Sweat makes his synthetic suit stick to his body like a second skin and he closes and opens his eyes, zeroing in. Fans in the stands jump, cheer, and yell, but he turns his ears off to everything but the engine and his breath. A few minutes until *go,*and he's calm.

He grips the wheel, tapping his toe slowly, patiently counting down each red light as it extinguishes. Tap…tap…tap. The engine revs and his gaze fixates on the road. Accelerate.

Most racing experts consider Mario Andretti to be one of the most successful professional racers of all time. In his prime, he won the Daytona 500, Indianapolis 500, Formula One World Championship, and the Pikes Peak International Hill Climb. Andretti is one of only two drivers in history to win races in IndyCar, Formula One, World Sportscar Championship, and NASCAR.

When asked to share his number one tip for success on the racetrack, he said, "Don't look at the wall. Your car goes where your eyes go."[118]

Any driver can tell you they learned this lesson at a very young age. When they're learning to drive at two hundred miles per hour, they are taught to focus on the road in front of them. The number one rookie mistake is focusing on the wall because if you look at the wall, you hit it.

Focusing on the road, on your conception of your future, requires willpower to ignore the walls. Sometimes these walls are not as obvious as explicit naysayers or insurmountable logistical barriers; rather, they can be the walls in the car itself, the people you surround yourself with and trust. **Regardless of how fast you press the accelerator, if the walls are too fragile, they will hold you back.**

I came across this quote and thought to share it: **"You can't change the people around you, but you can change the people around you."**

---

118 Clear, James. 2013. "How To Deal With Judgment And Criticism In A Healthy Way". 2013. *Lifehacker Australia*. Accessed November 8 2018. https://www.lifehacker.com.au/2013/10/how-to-deal-with-judgment-and-criticism-in-a-healthy-way/.

At first glance, it seems like a riddle my middle school English teacher would put on a test as extra credit. But of course, after a bit more thought, the message becomes clear. Your inner circle and whoever is in it either hurts or helps you. Often times, those closest may be the ones rooting against you, and the reason why is simple. People who put forth an extra effort to achieve their ambitions tend to make others, who don't, insecure.

Consider this story from Shivaram Kumar, a serial entrepreneur, author, motivational speaker, and father of three pretty cool daughters *wink wink* has a great anecdote about this.

Papa grew up in Chembur, Mumbai, in a rented one-room and kitchen apartment with his two sisters and parents. In his building, there was a patch of green—a small rectangular play area surrounded on three sides by the building and the fourth a street. They called this oasis the "compound." At the center of the compound was a beautiful budding mango tree, which belonged to the landlord. Every summer, my dad and his friend would throw rocks and stones at the tree to dislodge the mangoes.

Usually, their tiny, agile bodies outran the old landlord, but one day, my Thatha (grandfather) caught them. He said, in Tamil, "I know we're not rich, son. But we can afford to buy mangoes from the market." My dad wanted to tell him that he felt a special thrill in breaking open stolen mangoes and squinting at the brisk sourness of the mud-stained pieces.

When I heard this story when I was younger, I thought that its moral was that stolen mangoes taste better. But my dad quickly corrected me.

"Nobody throws stones at trees with no fruit. Any tree bearing fruit can expect to have to withstand some trouble."

He goes further to elaborate.

"There are two spheres in life—things you can control, and things you can't. So often people spend their time worrying about things they can't control, like fantasy football or the weather or what someone says to them. We can't control what others say. We can only control how we react. Our thoughts, feelings, and actions are in our control. So if you're succeeding, and others are throwing stones at you, you can control who you listen to."

I heard this story when I was very young, and it prompted me to look closely at who was throwing stones at me. I noticed people who I consider friends saying things like, "Why are you so uptight? You're young. Let loose," when I stayed in weekends to work on my book.

One of my friends feels a similar thing when she sticks to her rigorous gym schedule.

"Some people are threatened when others do the things they wished they could do."

The second I realized who in my life is making these comments that distract and belittle me, I create distance. And I'm not the only one who does this. Manu "Swish" Goswami, twenty-year-old Canadian serial entrepreneur, talked about how he, through redefining himself, had to redefine his inner circle as well.

His head buried in his books, messy hair flopping over his glasses to focus his gaze like blinders on a horse, Swish passed hour after hour studying in the library. He mastered school with a tremendous work ethic that led him to get 100 percent on all of his tests and finish first in his class. Nobody thought that, only a year after graduating, he'd take a gap year from school and become an entrepreneur. "When I was younger, I got called 'nerd' a lot of times. Now I'm not even in school." Ten years ago, nobody at his school thought he would ever do what he's doing now.

"The people around me had to make a decision. Are they going to see Swish as an entrepreneur or are they going to stop being his friend and not talk to him again?

"Some people chose the latter, and a lot of people chose the former. And those are the people I continue to cater to and care about and love."

Swish articulated beautifully what I didn't know I knew. When your interests change from those around you, and they are no longer compatible with who you want to be, you have to refine your inner circle. Only then do you free yourself to pursue your ambition wholeheartedly. Only then will you play tag with people in your league.

In order to take an honest look at your personal network, or "egonetwork" in network theory, it's important to visualize it. So, this next part explains how I visualize the relationships that surround me.

ATOMIC ORBITALS (WARNING: NERD PARAGRAPH)

Yes, I'm a nerd. So I'm going to use this as an opportunity to present my atomic model of personal networks, a theory I developed to explain our relationship with those around us.

Our personal networks can be represented by a variation of Bohr's atomic model, proposed by Danish physicist Niels Bohr in 1913. Below I have attached a simplistic image of an atom illustrating the model. Note that neither my nor Bohr's model is 100 percent accurate; it's just a framework I chose to use to analyze my Egonetwork.

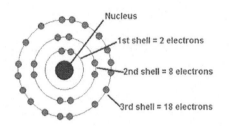

119

You see here the nucleus, made up of neutrons and protons, which together create a positive charge.

The grey dots are negatively charged electrons, which are locked into fixed orbits around the nucleus and therefore have fixed energies. (It's slightly more complicated, but this was Bohr's theory.)

According to Bohr, the electrons can only change orbits by quantum leaps, or fixed amounts, from one orbit to another. The circles around the nucleus are known as energy shells, which are made up of groups of orbitals of equivalent energy (not pictured).

119 Ramakrishnan, Dinesh. 2018. "What Are The Drawbacks Of Bohr's Theory?". *Infofavour.Blogspot.Com*. Accessed November 8 2018. https://infofavour.blogspot.com/2014/06/what-are-drawbacks-of-bohrs-theory.html.

Essentially, each orbital can hold at most two electrons, and each shell can hold at most $2n2$ electrons, where n=number of level. For example, the second level can hold $2x22=8$ electrons, as shown in the image.

Basically, atoms are mostly empty space with a positively charged nucleus surrounded by electrons that travel in circular orbits. The lower the energy level, the closer the electrons are to the positively charged nucleus and the harder the nucleus pulls on them.

How does this apply to my ego network? Well, the nucleus, as the center of the atom, represents me and people who I believe are so essential to my identity that I would be a fundamentally different person without. In my life, this is my direct family: Mom, Dad, Tarika, Ritika. The first energy level contains only the orbital with the two people outside of my nucleus closest to me, and as the energy levels increase, the orbitals distance themselves but include more people. In its simplest form, the atomic model and its ring of concentric circles can be used to explain the levels of closeness in my friendships.

But a closer look at the chemistry reveals some more nuanced implications.

When light interacts with matter, it can either be absorbed or emitted. Albert Einstein discovered that an electron can only be ejected from the atom by interacting with one photon at a time. A photon is essentially a quantum of light. The system has to conserve energy, so when an atom absorbs light, an electron jumps to an orbit further from the nucleus and the atom increases its potential energy.

Bohr's model helps me understand that refining my inner circle requires surrounding myself with people who add to the potential energy of the system. The only real way to get rid of someone negative in your inner circle is to absorb a lot of light and positivity from the external world, often enough to push an electron further away. The brighter the light, the more electrons jump further away from the nucleus.

When you absorb all the light and push the negativity out further, you're left with so much potential energy to go out and play productively with your network and even expand your network.

EXPANDING YOUR CIRCLES

We saw earlier how one weak tie between two groups that exhibit homophily is a great opportunity to gain access to information you wouldn't have been able to access without that tie. *Networks, Crowds, and Markets* sums it up well with the following quote.

"The argument is that these are the social ties that connect us to new sources of information and new opportunities, and their conceptual 'span' in the social network (the local bridge property) is directly related to their weakness as social ties. This dual role as weak connections but also valuable conduits to hard-to-reach parts of the network—this is the surprising strength of weak ties."[120]

My version of play is going out and talking to strangers. I play by meeting new people, and I'm not scared of it? Why? Because I know that even though we're more connected than ever before, people are still lonely. Cigna surveyed twenty thousand adults and found that 54 percent of respondents said they feel like no one actually knows them well. Forty percent said they "lack companionship," "their relationships aren't meaningful," and that they feel "isolated from others."[121]

It's like when two restaurants are across the street from one another. There are a lot of people in one and barely any in

---

120 Easley, David, and Jon Kleinberg. 2018. *Networks, Crowds, And Markets*. Johanneshov: MTM.

121 Jenkins, Aric. "Survey Finds That Half of Americans – Especially Young People – Feel Lonely". 2018. *Fortune*. Accessed November 8 2018. http://fortune.com/2018/05/01/americans-lonely-cigna-study/.

the other, so most of us assume that the crowded one is better. We assume that the people inside that restaurant know something that we don't. But this might not be the case, as everyone on the inside could have made their decision like we did.

Similarly, when we see someone texting on the subway, we assume they're not lonely. *They're talking to a friend or doing important work.* But they usually want to meet new people too.

I no longer make those kinds of assumptions. I understand just how beneficial weak ties can be, so I add a fourth level of tagging—tagging someone you don't know.

***

Tag is all about taking advantage of our hyperconnectivity and interconnectedness today. When you play tag, you rely on relationships and networks to inspire you to think differently and innovate confidently. You can interact with weak ties and strong ties—ultimately, Tag is really about letting others push you to push yourself. It's an incredible way to play because you end up with best friends who inspire you to live up to your potential.

CHAPTER 7

COLOR OUTSIDE

———

My legs curl, crunched behind the seat in front of me, and I lose feeling in my feet. My little sister plops her heavy head on my shoulder, so I bid sleep a bitter farewell and plug my headphones in to watch the newest animation-sensation, *Coco*.

Main character Miguel starts telling his story of his secret love for music, a love forbidden by his family of music-haters. The movie progresses, and I follow Miguel on his journey through the land of the dead to discover his family history, wiping tears and celebrating along the way. I won't spoil the ending , as my friend Anna always does for me, but you should watch this movie for its brilliant portrayal of Mexican folklore, family, and friendship.

Who thought to make this movie? The same people who thought of a hilariously forgetful sidekick fish helping a desperate father find his lost son in the vast ocean and the same people who imagined how a toy cowboy and an astronaut develop a deep friendship when nobody's watching.

Adults make these movies, and each movie is so creative and captivating, so there's no way it's a fluke. Pixar has created a reputation for itself, bolstered by every new movie in its endless stream of unique stories, as the most creative computer animation force.

How?

Pixar's leaders have discovered potent practices for operating and structuring a creative organization, practices we can learn from. They have learned how to construct an environment of innovation, one that unleashes the creativity of each individual. Having talented people is certainly part of it, but the magic ingredient is more than that.

***

Color Outside: Play by crossing the boundaries between disciplines. The best approach to problem-solving is an interdisciplinary one. Thinking like someone you don't surround yourself with increases your empathy and understanding for the world around you.

Interdisciplinary often involves collaboration and serendipity. While it can be hard to run into interdisciplinarity if the infrastructure is not in place, the effort involved in actively seeking out interdisciplinary connections is worth it. You can color inside during the nine-to-five or outside the nine-to-five. Either way, doing so will catalyze learning and creativity exponentially.

***

Pixar understands the untapped potential that lives in inter-disciplinary connections.

Danielle Feinberg, in her Ted Talk, talks about how she brings Pixar movies to life – using lighting.[122]

Take Finding Nemo, for example. A majority of the film takes place underwater, but how did she create the underwater illusion?

---

122 Feinberg, Danielle. 2018. "The Magic Ingredient That Brings PixarMovies To Life". Ted.Com. Accessed November 8 2018. https://www.ted.com/talks/danielle_feinberg_the_magic_ingredient_that_brings_pixar_movies_to_life?language=en.

While in the R&D phase of he film, she took a clip of underwater footage and recreated it on a computer. Then she and her team broke it down to see the elements that create the underwater aesthetic, and she realized light was a big part of it. She then created code to mimic the physics of light passing through water and how color changes as you go deeper into the water. The surge and swell creates that invisible underwater current that pushes bits of particulate around the water, the caustics create those ribbons of light rippling across the screen, the fog beams give color depth and signal where the surface of the ocean is.

"You can see how we're using science—the physics of water, light, and movement—to tether artistic freedom." Artistic freedom, while an incredible thing that allows them to create any world they can conceive of, can create chaos. So, a combination of both science and artistic vision allows Danielle and Pixar to push our perception of reality to the ideal level of unrealistically realistic. "We use science to create something wonderful. We use story and artistic touch to get us to a place of wonder."[123]

Danielle, and Pixar as a whole, understand just how key combining disciplines is in igniting innovation.

---

123 Ibid.

WHERE INNOVATION OCCURS

The old building smelled like moldy carpet and the thin walls held eerie memories from their time as an overflow World War II shelter. Located at the intersection of Main and Vassar Streets in East Cambridge, Massachusetts, the building housed overflow from MIT's Radiation Laboratory. But even when the war ended, instead of demolishing the "failed" Building 20, MIT continued to use the space for overflow.

"The result was that a mismatch of different departments—from nuclear science to linguistics to electronics—shared the low-slung building alongside more ordinary tenants such as a machine shop and a piano repair facility. Because the building was cheaply constructed, these groups felt free to rearrange the space as needed. Walls and floors could be shifted and equipment bolted to the beams. For instance, a scientist working on the first atomic clock removed two floors from his Building 20 lab so he could install the three-story cylinder needed for his experiments."[124]

Cal Newport, author of *Deep Work,* worked in Building 20 during his seven years at MIT. According to Cal, it is generally accepted that this "haphazard combination of different disciplines," thrown together blindly in a loosely-structured building led to a boom of ingenuity and constant, creative

---

124 Newport, Cal. 2016. *Deep Work.*

innovation. Chomsky grammars, Loran navigational radars, and video games, all emerged from within the walls of Building 20.[125]

Cal offers another inspiring building design to help further illustrate: Bell Labs tower in Murray Hill, New Jersey.

Director Mervin Kelly designed the building so that it would intentionally mix together scientists and engineers. Instead of following the standard model housing different departments in different buildings, he "connected the spaces into one contiguous structure joined by long hallways—some so long that when you stood at one end it would appear to converge to a vanishing point." One employee remarked that walking down the hall without running into acquaintances, problems, diversions and ideas was almost impossible.[126]

Like Building 20, Bell Labs became a cauldron bubbling with innovation. For example, the lab produced the first cellular communication system, solar cell, laser, communication satellite, and fiber optic networking, to name a few.

"At the same time, their theorists formulated both information theory and coding theory, their astronomers won the

---

125 Ibid.
126 Ibid.

Nobel Prize for empirically validating the Big Bang Theory, and perhaps most important of all, their physicists invented the transistor," Cal adds.[127]

So, what caused this "spirit of inventiveness?" What spurs these breakthroughs?

STRUCTURED SERENDIPITY

When I interviewed Cal, he told me that it all came down to "chance encounters between people of different disciplines." He expounded to introduce his term of "serendipitous creativity." Serendipitous creativity refers to what happens when people bump into each other, causing smart collaborations and new ideas to emerge.

Entrepreneur Frans Johansson described this phenomenon as the "Medici effect," referring to the creative explosion in Florence when the Medici family brought together people from a wide range of disciplines—sculptors, scientists, poets, philosophers, painters, and architects. As these individuals connected, new ideas blossomed at the intersections of their respective fields, thereby spawning the Renaissance, one of the most inventive eras in history.[128]

---

127 Ibid.
128 Johansson, Frans. 2006. *The Medici Effect*. Boston, Mass.: Harvard Business School Press.

So many inventions were unlikely to have arisen simply due to the work of a single person in a single department. Having someone else around with a fresh perspective and a complementary skillset really helps. Cal articulates the value someone else can add in a blog he wrote:

Working with someone else at a proverbial whiteboard can push you deeper than if you were working alone. The presence of the other party waiting for your next insight—be it someone physically in the same room or collaborating with you virtually—can short-circuit the natural instinct to avoid depth.[129]

Here's another more ~mathematical~ way to look at it: while most people think that great ideas come with an increase in expertise, the relationship between insight and expertise is not exactly linear; it's more of a bell curve.

French mathematician Adolphe Quetelet first noticed this trend in the 19th century. Quetelet studied the careers of playwrights and graphed their productivity over time. He found that most playwrights produced output upwards until hitting a creative peak, at which point their productivity decreased.[130]

---

129 Newport, Cal. 2016. *Deep Work*.
130 Scientists, Top, and List Scientists. 2018. "Adolphe Quetelet". *Famousscientists.Org*. Accessed November 8 2018. https://www.famousscientists.org/adolphe-quetelet/.

This is likely because as experts grow in their field, their opinions about what won't work grow. They know more precedent, so they won't retest ideas that have failed in the past. An outsider, on the other hand, has enough expertise to generate an idea but not enough to dismiss it untried.

HOW STRUCTURE AND FUNCTION LEAPFROG

"Most buildings are designed for some functional purpose, but ours is designed to maximize inadvertent encounters," says Ed Catmull, CEO of Pixar.[131]

When Steve Jobs (people forget he was the CEO of Pixar for a while!) was designing the headquarters for Pixar, he gave architects Bohlin, Cywinsky, and Jackson a simple instruction: make a design that "promoted encounters and unplanned collaborations."[132]

At the time, in the 1990s, film studios still had the cardboard office layouts. But the architects heeded Jobs' request and created an atrium with focal points such as a cafe, foosball table, and fitness center. The office has an Olympic-sized pool,

---

131 Catmull, Ed. 2008. "How Pixar Fosters Collective Creativity". 2008. *Harvard Business Review. Accessed November 8 2018. https://hbr. org/2008/09/how-pixar-fosters-collective-creativity.*

132 Bell, Chris. 2013. "Monsters University: What's It Like To Work At Pixar? ". *Telegraph.Co.Uk. Accessed November 8 2018. https://www. telegraph.co.uk/culture/film/10144531/Monsters-University-whats-it-like-to-work-at-Pixar.html.*

football field, basketball court, and more. Pixar's chefs even have their own organic vegetable garden on the campus. Perhaps equally importantly, like outside, there is freedom inside. Offices have Wawa hours and employees can come and go according to their own schedule.[133]

Sure, some people may not exactly maximize the potential of the freedom they have been granted…

People like Phil Shoebottom, a lighting director at Pixar, certainly experienced some abuse of freedom.

"I remember when I started thinking it was the strangest place I'd ever seen," he says. "One morning there was a half-naked guy standing on a table in the cafeteria, playing the saxophone. Or you'd leave to go to your car in the evening, and there'd be a ballroom dancing class in the atrium. At the start you feel British about it, but you can't help but get sucked in."

And Paul Oakley, another lighting director, had a similar experience.

"There's something different every day. When we started working on *Monsters University*, everyone had to join a fraternity. My hazing process involved me dressing up as Mrs.

---

133 Ibid.

Doubtfire for the day. I had to go to a director review in full makeup. But someone else was dressed as Tinky Winky from Teletubbies, so that was okay."[134]

While the freedom may have resulted in odd or unpredictable encounters, people certainly made the most of it. The collaboration and intellectual freedom to traverse the disciplines led Pixar to the top of the movie animation game.

We've heard the saying, "form follows function," which is a 20th century architecture quote that says that the shape of a building or object should relate to its intended function. In other words, when designing a building, start with the purpose of a building.

Pixar is certainly a place with purpose.

There are only a few times in my life when I felt like my surroundings were structured for serendipitous creativity.

One place is the New Jersey Scholars Program, or NJSP. NJSP is a five-week summer program for 39 stellar NJ nerds interested in learning for the sake of learning. The program focuses on one topic – my year was *Climate Change and the Human Experience* – and examines it from four lenses:

---

134 Ibid.

Science, Anthropology, Religion/Politics, and Literature. There are no grades or graded homeworks, and there are no banal lectures for formality. Everything is seminar style – Harkness, to be specific – and the scholars, not the professors, dominate the conversation.

At NJSP, I surrounded myself with people who were passionate about everything from legal chemistry to epigenetics, and collided with their ideas on a daily basis. We worked together to examine problems, combining our relative expertises to arrive at a holistic understanding of what we were learning. We played with ideas every day, generating unlikely combinations that even resulted in starting new businesses and initiatives. It was intellectual recess, and it was insanely fun.

I went back to NJSP this past summer, the summer before my third year of college, as a program assistant and housemaster. I had a job in NYC for 11 weeks, but I commuted for five of them from NJSP. I worked at NJSP from 7pm-7am and in NYC from 9am-6pm. While I dreaded the commute, I loved being immersed in NJSP's environment, one structured for serendipitous creativity, once again. Nothing had changed since I attended: people entered heated philosophical debates at 2am, extreme liberals and extreme conservatives *shared* their politics and became best friends, and the aroma of interdisciplinarity filled the halls.

But places like Pixar and NJSP are exceptions. Apart from these few and far between settings intended for interdisciplinary collisions and designed for "coloring outside," collaborating with others requires a lot of individual effort.

In other words, I usually have to carry my coloring book with me to places where you're not supposed to and forge my own interdisciplinary journey. I learned to make connections when nobody asked me to. And it's been more than worth it.

HOW TO COLOR OUTSIDE AT SCHOOL

We know that an interdisciplinary approach propels creativity, drives innovation, and maximizes learning. But how can we color outside when people hide the crayons and tell you to just print out a picture instead?

I've been in school most of my life, and I am fortunate enough to have genuinely enjoyed school. At Montessori school, I was in a class of thirty students, ten in each grade. We all shared a single classroom in which third grade math and first grade English occurred side-by-side, and there was no concept of disciplinary or physical separation.

In fourth grade, we separated into Math/Science and English/History, but our classes were still small. Then in middle school, we branched further into Math, Science, English, and Social Studies. You can guess what's next, but come ninth grade we had a whole new assortment of specialties and levels based on preference and academic achievement.

Even with the increased options, you still pretty much had to take one science, one math, one English, and one history for all four years, which balanced out your exposure. But then here comes college, and we have to pick one thing to major in. Depending on what school you go to, and whether it has a core curriculum, you can pretty much stay in your chosen lane for four years. I illustrate branching of specialization that happens as you progress through the education system diagram my sister, Tarika (thank you so much!), created for me below.

Subject Matter at Stages of the American Education System

Kindergarten	All Subjects							
Elementary School	Math/Science				English/History			
Middle School	Math		Science		English		Social Studies	
High School Courses	Geometry	Algebra	Biology	Chemistry	AP Lit	Shakespeare	US History	AP Gov
	AP BC Calculus	Trigonometry	Physics	Computer Science	AP Lang	Creative Writing	Comp. Gov	Cold War History
University Majors	Accounting	Logic	Engineering	Psychology	Philosophy	Journalism	Politics	Economics
	Statistics	Discrete Mathematics	Pre-Med	Health Studies	Marketing	Communications	Pre-Law	Philosophy

This increase in specialization certainly has its merits, as it allows for the creation of expertise and the pursuit of niche interests. But it also creates more points of divergence between you and someone who studies in a sibling or parent of your chosen subject.

In other words, it is rather likely that a Spanish literature major might meet and exchange ideas with an English major because they may share a prerequisite class or have class in the same building. But how often do pre-med students meet finance majors? How often does a history major have a conversation with a nursing major?

In college, those conversations happen largely outside of the classroom. You meet people with other interests by joining clubs, through random friends, or at parties. Depending on your major, your "nine-to-five" your time could be mostly spent around people who have taken the same classes as you and have the same interests as you so much so that they approach problems like you do.

This stratification and segmentation based on specialization often makes people feel claustrophobic, stifled, or not unique. You can restore a sense of individuality by being the different one in the room—a big part of reigniting individual creativity revolves around deliberately exposing yourself to the unfamiliar.

CROSS-ASSOCIATION

Associating, or the ability to successfully connect seemingly unrelated questions, problems, or ideas from different fields, is central to the innovator's DNA.[135] Cross-Association requires opening your mind to think about things broadly.

Here is a glimpse into my mind as a tenth grader (if you're curious), before I was asked to choose one thing to specialize in college, actually an excerpt from my application to NJSP.

In my tenth grade English class, I delved into the mind of young Hamlet by analyzing his famous "to be or not to be" soliloquy, in which Hamlet considers taking his own life. At the same time, I had been watching a Spanish film entitled Mar Adentro, which was based off of the life of Ramón Sampedro, a quadriplegic debating whether or not to get euthanized . Even though his family and friends encouraged him to stay alive, he felt living wasn't worth it.

When I studied polarity in chemistry, how some molecules can have a positive or negative charge, I learned that structure affects function. If even one atom in a molecule is omitted,

---

135 Dyer, Jennifer. "The Innovator'S DNA". 2009. *Harvard Business Review*. Accessed November 8 2018. https://hbr.org/2009/12/the-innovators-dna.

*the entire molecule can be destroyed. If the fate of an entity
is determined by the actions of each element of that entity,
shouldn't each element work carefully to assure functionality?
Do people experiencing suicidal thoughts consider the effects
their deaths could have on the people around them?*

I began asking these questions in the tenth grade and continued to explore. And I credit my sophomore year Honors
Chemistry class for inspiring them. Our teacher, Dr. Gadd,
gave us freedom to investigate. The excitement with which
he explained the material, the camaraderie of my classmates
during 3 a.m. study sessions, and the scope of the curriculum
– not tailored to any predetermined blueprint – inspired me
to meditate on the concepts of chemistry beyond the context
of the class.

Once you develop an inclination to think across the disciplines, you can do it deliberately and often.

Pixar—surprise, surprise—gives us a good idea about what
cross-association looks like. Co-Founder Ed Catmull of Pixar
not only recognizes that the barriers between disciplines are
"impediments to producing great work," but also does "everything he can to tear them down."[136]

---

136 Catmull, Ed. 2008. "How Pixar Fosters Collective Creativity". 2008.
*Harvard Business Review. Accessed November 8 2018. https://hbr.
org/2008/09/how-pixar-fosters-collective-creativity.*

One salient example of an interdisciplinary effort is Pixar University, which offers a broad range of courses open to anyone in any discipline to take. Some, like screenplay and sculpting, are directly related to work, and some, like yoga and Pilates, are not. In these classes, there are novices and experts, because Pixar wants to emphasize that "we're all learning and it's fun to learn together."[137]

In school, we have all the options and materials we need to create our own version of Pixar University. You just have to game the system. You have to become a transnational force and develop special relations with different, perhaps even warring, countries, so you can cross borders with ease and amnesty.

I have been gaming the system ever since I was forced to take required classes I had no interest in. Wiggling my way into courses I didn't technically qualify for became a game for me and enabled me to create my own interdisciplinary education, which is pretty awesome. Honestly, that's probably part of the reason why I use so many math and science analogies in this book.

It became a little harder in college, when I was forced to pick a major. But I wiggled my way out of the trap and made

---

137 Ibid.

my own interdisciplinary major. I researched similar majors at other schools, particularly Stanford University and the University of Pennsylvania, memorized Georgetown course offerings, and pitched a 20-page proposal to my Dean.

I was paying thousands of dollars to study here, so I should be able to take whatever I want, right?

In this process, I discovered a passion for network analysis and graph theory, connected with professors in all kinds of departments – business, mathematics, physcology, and more – and changed my environment so it would prioritize cross-association.

I gamed the system so I can continue to pinpoint untouched intersections between disparate disciplines.

If you're in college, game the system. That's how you'll learn more, and that's how you'll innovate.

Go to professors in various disciplines, professors who teach classes restricted to people of a certain major with certain prerequisites, and make a case for yourself. Even if you're not in college and confined to some other rigid, in-the-lines structure, game the system. Make friends in other departments at work. Use lunch to take an online class in accounting. Volunteer your services pro bono on a new project.

***

At Pixar, regardless of your title, you have a voice. That's why every single person—from animators to lighting directors to screenwriters, and to accountants—who works at the studio is in the credits. Monsters University director Dan Scanlon notes: "When we put a film out into the world, the whole studio is behind it."[138]

That's why Pixar makes such iconic films – because they promote interdisciplinary efforts.

Coloring outside has two parts:

1. Color outside the lines. Cross where you're not supposed to, blend where they don't tell you to.
2. Game the system by taking your coloring book with you everywhere you go. Create a culture of cross-associating on your own.

---

138 Bell, Chris. 2013. "Monsters University: What's It Like To Work At Pixar? ". *Telegraph.Co.Uk*. Accessed November 8 2018. https://www.telegraph.co.uk/culture/film/10144531/Monsters-University-whats-it-like-to-work-at-Pixar.html.

When Danielle Feinberg (from the beginning of this chapter) was seven, she proudly told an adult she wanted to be an artist. The adult said, "No you don't. You can't make a living being an artist!" So she settled on becoming a scientist.[139]

She uses math, science and code to create these amazing animated worlds. She uses storytelling and art to bring them to life. This interweaving of art and science elevates the world to a place of wonder, a place with soul, a place we can believe in, a place where the things you imagine can become real—and a place where a girl suddenly realizes not only is she a scientist, but also an artist.

If you play by coloring outside, you'll open up your mind to all sorts of connections and insights you never would have seen before. After you practice for a while, it gets harder and harder to parse through and segregate different thoughts; eventually, you see everything combine into one beautiful story about a fish underwater.

---

139 Feinberg, Danielle. 2018. "The Magic Ingredient That Brings Pixar Movies To Life". *Ted.Com. Accessed November 8 2018. https://www. ted.com/talks/danielle_feinberg_the_magic_ingredient_that_brings_ pixar_movies_to_life?language=en.*

CHAPTER 8

ON THE FIELD

———

Australian Open, 2017. Legs weak from hours in the Australian heat, Roger Federer played with balance and grace, carefully trying to limit the damage wrought by Nadal's powerful forehand. His crisp backhands fell right before the baseline, sending Nadal off balance. Nadal employed his extraordinarily deep angles, expanding the court to bait Federer to come into the net. Instead, Federer aced his serves, sent sharp winners piercing down the line, and stepped into the court to cut off Nadal's topspin on the rise—all culminating in a quick, delicate forehand that just barely clipped the line. The crowd went nuts.

The thirty-five-year-old Swiss won 6-4, 3-6, 6-1, 6-3 to claim his fifth Australian Open title and become the oldest Grand

Slam winner since Ken Rosewall in 1972.[140] After five sets in three hours and thirty-eight minutes of back and forth momentum shifts, outsmarting and anticipating, and stretching themselves further than we thought humanly possible, Roger Federer made history.

Federer was the underdog. He arrived seeded just seventeenth, having not played an official tournament for more than six months. The matches that led up to the final were far from easy; he scraped his way through three five-set matches in the final four rounds, defeating top players Tomas Berduch, Kei Nishikori, and Stan Wawrinka before meeting his friendly rival, Rafael Nadal, in the finals.[141]

Over the years, Nadal's wild lefty topspin fatigued Federer's singlehanded backhand, match after match. They had a 23-11 record, Nadal to Federer before that final, and Nadal had won all three meetings at the Australian Open. Roger hadn't beaten Nadal in a slam in almost a decade, giving us no reason to believe this encounter should be any different.

How did he do it?

---

140 Clarey, Christopher. 2017. "Roger Federer, Defying Age, Tops Rafael Nadal In Australian Open Final". *Nytimes.Com*. Accessed November 8 2018. https://www.nytimes.com/2017/01/29/sports/tennis/roger-federer-rafael-nadal-australian-open.html.
141 Ibid.

"I told myself to play free," Federer said. "You play the ball. You don't play the opponent. Be free in your head. Be free in your shots. Go for it. The brave will be rewarded here. I didn't want to go down just making shots, seeing forehands rain down on me from Rafa."[142]

Federer's secret is his attitude. He thinks in the moment and knows that tennis is as much a mental game as a physical one. His twenty-some years playing tennis have cultivated in him an unparalleled mastery of grit, resilience, strategy, and mental toughness that only playing a sport can teach.

Some things are only learnable outside the nine-to-five, through activities like sports. Hence, our final playground principle: *On the Field.*

***

On the Field: Activities—sports, music, art, travel—are a kind of play most of us are familiar with because they are *intended for play.*

When you're on the field, court, or stage, you're operating in the moment, improvising with your team, and constantly building your mental, and often physical, toughness. These

---

142 Ibid.

activities teach you discipline and grit while challenging you to solve problems with imagination and creativity. They often involve a coach who mentors you beyond the activity, imparting wisdom that translates to other aspects of life.

On the Field is about engaging in activities that involve your full person—body and mind—to learn. It also means seeing the world as a field on which you play and bringing all the things you learn on the field to the rest of the world.

***

Roger Federer is perhaps the most perfect human being to exist, and so while it might be unfair to try to live up to his standard, we can certainly learn from it and study how he got to be the amazing person he is today. (Federer, if you ever read this book, please be my friend.)

Those intangible qualities—like sportsmanship, mental toughness, and focus—often cannot be taught in school. I played sports my whole life—tennis, basketball, track, swimming, softball, lacrosse, mock trial (yes, it counts)—and I learned as much, if not more, from being out on the field or court than in class.

As Angela Duckworth, author of *Grit,* says in an interview with *Forbes*, that high achievers, "have a kind of endurance in their effort... It is not that they do not get disappointed, but they get back up again, and they are tirelessly working to get better. Perseverance. But there is also stamina in their interest. They are just never bored with what they do. They find it interesting and meaningful, and so they do not switch course a lot."[143]

She continues by adding, "One of the great tragedies of American education is that extracurricular activities are becoming marginalized."[144]

Extracurricular activities—sports and travel, specifically—are ways to play that cultivate the soft skills necessary to succeed in both team and individual settings.

In this chapter, we'll go over some of the ways these various activities contribute to not only learning, creativity, and connecting but also developing soft skills—the kind that develop your character into someone strong, focused, and resilient. Venturing out *on the field* requires a full-body effort and is therefore a new challenge, but if you can arrange to be out there as often as possible, you'll come back with renewed perspective and new skills.

---

143 High, Peter. 2018. "The Secret Ingredient Of Successful People And Organizations: Grit". *Forbes*. Accessed November 8 2018. https://www.forbes.com/sites/peterhigh/2016/05/23/the-secret-ingredient-of-successful-people-and-organizations-grit/#24ef19a262ef.
144 Ibid.

SPORTS AND BUSINESS

When Satya Nadella, CEO of Microsoft, was younger, his father put a poster of Karl Marx in his bedroom. His mother, a schoolteacher, hung a retaliation poster of Goddess Lakshmi, a Hindu deity representing wealth and contentment, on the other wall.

"The only poster I really wanted was one of my cricketing hero, the Hyderabadi great, ML Jaisimha, famous for his boyish good looks and graceful style, on and off the field," Nadella writes in his memoir, *Hit Refresh*.[145]

Nadella played cricket at his school and has spoken before about how the sport influenced his career. "On those fields, I learned a lot about myself...succeeding and failing as a bowler, a batsman, and a fielder. Even today I catch myself reflecting on the nuances within the cricket rulebook and the inherent grace of a team of eleven working together as one unit."[146]

Certainly, he knows how to run a cohesive unit. As CEO, Nadella spearheaded the shift to make Microsoft

---

145 Lebowitz, Shana. 2018. "A Single High School In India Has Produced The Ceos Of Microsoft, Adobe, And Mastercard". *Business Insider*. Accessed November 8 2018. https://www.businessinsider.com/microsoft-adobe-mastercard-ceos-went-to-same-high-school-2018-3?utm_content=buffer5366d&utm_medium=social&utm_source=facebook.com&utm_campaign=buffer-ti&fbclid=IwAR1vWbgWLcP9c1cch-vQ8giF_R9gzwoY35yzuw3VHhQ4PePdsS2qlCDXDjb8.
146 Ibid.

a cloud-computing giant through its Azure platform. Nadella has also orchestrated some big moves for Microsoft, most notably its $26.2 billion acquisition of LinkedIn.

He credits a lot of his success now to his early years playing cricket. In an interview with Wharton Business School, Nadella said he learned from his high school cricket coach how to walk the line "between having confidence in your own capability yet having the ability to learn."

He distills three top lessons he learned from cricket that translated to his business success:

- **Have Respect for the Competition**. One time, Nadella was playing a fairly intimidating Australian team. His coach yelled at them, encouraging their captain to play with some aggression. Nadella was put at the forward short leg position, right beside the scariest Australian batsman. This story taught him how to respect the competitor without being afraid.
- **Prioritize the Team**. A teammate of his was an exceptionally fast bowler, one "of the best in the land." But he had a self-destructive mindset. Once when he was moved to a position he didn't like, he purposefully missed an easy catch. Lesson? One bad character with an ego can ruin the whole team's effort.
- **Be an Empathetic Leader**. One match, Nadella's bowling was getting obliterated by the opponents. His serve was ordinary and unexceptional, so his captain took Nadella out of the

game and took his place. As anyone does when they replace the bowler, the captain took the wicket, signaling he would replace Nadella for a while. But instead of doing so, the captain immediately let Nadella back in the game, displaying faith in his teammate's ability. From this story, Nadella learned that leaders invest in building up their teammates. The best leaders bolster the confidence of the ones they are leading.[147]

And Nadella isn't the only one who has reaped the benefits of participating in sports at an early age:

- Indra Nooyi, Chairman and CEO of PepsiCo, played cricket at college in India.
- Mark Zuckerberg, CEO of Facebook, was captain of his high school fencing team.
- Meg Whitman, former CEO of Hewlett Packard Enterprise, was a competitive swimmer and also played lacrosse, tennis, and basketball.
- Walter Robb, former co-CEO of Whole Foods, was the captain of the Stanford Soccer Team.
- Brian Moynihan, Chairman and CEO of Bank of America, played rugby at Brown University.

Vin McCaffrey, CEO of Game Theory Group, an organization that helps student athletes transition to the workplace

---

147 Ibid.

and matches them with potential employers, says that the secret to winning in corporate leadership is understanding winning and losing.

Athletes understand this naturally.

"People don't hire student athletes because they're stars on a football field," he says. "What we find in every type of employment engagement is that there are certain traits employers desire—persistence, time management, communication skills, determination, internal motivation. You can't find that kid in the economics class. You find him or her in athletics," McCaffrey continues.[148]

Athletes develop skills that employers want. According to two recent studies published in the *Journal of Leadership & Organizational Studies*, 43 percent of high school students in the United States who have played sports tended to have more leadership, self-confidence, and self-respect. The study also found that even those who played high school sports fifty years ago showed higher (actual) leadership, self-confidence, and self-respect.[149]

148 Mcaffrey, Vin. "GTG Featured In EY Women Athletes & ESPNW Study – Game Plan". 2015. *Game Plan.* Accessed November 8 2018. http://wearegameplan.com/blog/gtg-featured-in-ey-women-athletes-espnw-study/.

149 Sugar, Rachel. 2018. "Researchers Have A Theory To Explain Why High-School Athletes Go On To Be Successful In Life". *Business*

Of course, you can develop these skills and traits without playing sports. The point here is to notice the correlation between developing desirable qualities and participating in sports. These qualities make you more equipped to succeed both in formal business settings and in less structured ways, like entrepreneurship.

ENTREPRENEURSHIP

Countless stories tell of former athletes bringing their love of competition and risk-taking to the tech industry, and one of the brightest examples is Jason Fox, former NFL player for the Miami Dolphins and Detroit Lions.

Fox grew up in Fort Worth, Texas, where he enjoyed the simple, but important, things in life: sports, country music, and family. Fox founded EarBuds, a real-time social music platform that lets users listen to songs with friends anywhere in the world and communicate on a mobile app.

"The idea of Earbuds actually came when I was a player," he says in an interview with *Forbes*, "and I watched Cam Newton warming up across the field jamming with his headphones

---

Insider. Accessed November 8 2018. https://www.businessinsider.com/why-athletes-make-good-employees-2015-6.

on. I thought, man, I wish I could tune into that! Now I am making that possible."[150]

Fox makes a good point here. Playing sports itself gets you expert experience in a new industry and therefore close access to niche problems you can solve. Take, for example, the story of Sunniva Super Coffee, founded by the DiCicco brothers: Jordan, who had a full scholarship at Philadelphia University for basketball, James, who played on the football team at Georgetown University, and Jim, who was the captain of Colgate football team.

Jordan, while still enrolled in college at Philadelphia University, came up with the business idea after reaching the brink of exhaustion. His brother, Jimmy, explains, "He had 5 a.m. basketball practices, a full day of classes, and late nights at the library... He was tired, as you can imagine. He was out of energy and his school store offered the traditional bottled coffee and energy drinks. Loaded with sugars and unhealthy ingredients, it didn't really give him the energy he was looking for."[151]

---

150 Hall, Mark. 2018. "From Athlete To Entrepreneur: An Interview About Why The Tech Industry Attracts So Many Sports Stars". *Forbes.* Accessed November 8 2018. https://www.forbes.com/sites/markhall/2018/04/17/from-athlete-to-entrepreneur/#55bb3d2456c8.

151 Menayang, Adi. 2017. "The Brothers Behind Sunniva Super Coffee Tap Into Student Demand For More Energy". 2017. *Foodnavigator-Usa.Com.* Accessed November 8 2018.

At the same time, a recipe for Bulletproof Coffee, a mixture of coffee, butter, and a special kind of oil, was going viral online. Jordan took that basic template, replaced butter with coconut fat, and added milk protein isolate to make the coffee creamy. He began sharing it with his teammates and coaches, "and before long, he had a profitable business out of his dorm room."

The brothers combined forces to capitalize on Jordan's idea and founded Sunniva in 2015. In their first year, they landed deals at Whole Foods, local chains and independent stores, and college campuses such as Georgetown, Princeton, Rutgers, and George Washington University, amounting to a total 150 points of sale.

"We sold over 200,000 bottles of coffee last year," Jimmy said. "We're proving that people want this."[152]

Because Jordan was a serious basketball player, he had specific dietary restrictions preventing him from using any of the coffee products on the market. His experience with sports illuminated a common problem overworked college athletes share and put him in a position to innovate and address it.

https://www.foodnavigator-usa.com/Article/2017/04/04/
Sunniva-Super-Coffee-taps-into-student-demand-for-more-energy#.
152 Ibid.

Sunniva Super Coffee is shooting to hit $5 million in 2018 revenue.[153]

For Jason Fox and the Sunniva brothers, playing sports exposed them to more problems to solve.

POWER WOMEN PLAY SPORTS

Beth Brooke was told she may never walk again. Her teenage self heard the doctors diagnose a degenerative hip disease but didn't accept it. She made a promise to herself that she would not only walk but run, that she would become one of the best young athletes in the world.

A study conducted by EY Women Athletes Business Network and ESPNW surveyed more than four hundred female executives in five countries. The results show that upward of 94 percent of female executives played sports. Of these, more than half (52 percent) played at the university level, compared to 39 percent of women at lower management levels. The same study also surveyed female Fortune 500 executives and found that 80 percent played competitive sports.[154]

---

153 Ibid.

154 Fondas, Nanette. "Research: More Than Half Of Top Female Execs Were College Athletes". 2014. *Harvard Business Review*. Accessed November 8 2018. https://hbr.org/2014/10/research-more-than-half-of-female-execs-were-college-athletes.

So Brooke did just that and ended up playing Division 1 college basketball at Purdue University. She is now the global vice chair of Public Policy at Ernst & Young, not to mention one of the world's one hundred most powerful women. She told *Forbes* that basketball taught her discipline, focus, and teamwork.

Weili Dai, tech superstar who cofounded Marvell Technology Group in 1995 with annual revenues of $3.6 billion, also emphasizes how basketball prepared her to take over the world.

"The basketball court is the foundation for everything," she said. It taught her to strategize creatively, improvise to changing circumstance, and have a positive attitude. Basketball "allowed me in the business world to work 24/7."[155]

Sure, this makes sense, given that we just assessed the personal traits that sports help to develop. What's especially poignant here is how sports help women break gender norms—often a key hurdle to pass when reaching an executive position.

A United Nations report writes that "the participation of women and girls in sports challenges gender stereotypes and

---

155 Ibid.

discrimination, and can therefore be a vehicle to promote gender equality and the empowerment of women and girls. In particular, women in sports leadership can shape attitudes toward women's capabilities as leaders and decision-makers, especially in traditionally male domains."[156]

Sports teach young women and girls skills beyond teamwork and dedication. Sports teach them to be aggressive, competitive, and confrontational.

I'm no CEO (yet) but even I have found that my experience playing sports has made it easier to relate to and compete with men. I've played almost every sport—basketball, tennis, swimming, golf, softball, lacrosse, track and field, horseback riding, gymnastics—and while I didn't realize it at the time, they all helped me become more authoritative in my own eyes and in the eyes of others.

When I was the only girl playing pickup basketball during recess at school (or even now in college), there were two kinds of people on the court: 1) the person who tiptoed around me, afraid my delicate body would crumble when faced with aggressive defense, throwing me pity passes just to include me and 2) the person who saw how fast I could cut to open

---

156 "Women 2000 and Beyond."2018. *Un.Org.* Accessed November 8 2018. http://www.un.org/womenwatch/daw/public/Women%20and%20 Sport.pdf.

myself up to shots just inside the three, shots I'd make the majority of the time. There was always a mix of boys on the court, and all I needed was one of the boys from the second category to be on my team.

When I first started playing, my hands would shake when I got the ball, out of fear that I'd mess up and embarrass myself. I hesitated to dribble and immediately looked to pass. I'd run around on the court almost aimlessly, as if I was just there for show.

One day, I was shooting around with some guys, and we made bets on shots. "If I make this, you do ten pushups," kind of thing. One after the other, I made them sweat. I didn't miss a single shot. Proving them wrong was probably the greatest rush of adrenaline I've ever experienced. Now, I play without thinking. I compete with people regardless of how they see me on the court, playing for the sake of the game.

If I feel this rush of confidence on the court, I can only imagine what powerful women feel in the boardroom.

MOVEMENT AND CREATIVITY

"Sit as little as possible. Do not believe any idea that was not born in the open air and of free movement—in which the muscles do not also revel." ~ Nietzsche

A 2014 Stanford University study reinforced Nietzsche's point when it concluded that walking boosted creative inspiration.[157]

The study placed participants in different conditions: walking indoors on a treadmill, or sitting outdoors while being pushed in a wheelchair. Then, the researchers gave participants an object and told them to think of as many uses as they could for that object. An idea was deemed novel if it was reasonable and if nobody else thought of that same idea.

"The overwhelming majority of the participants in these... experiments were more creative while walking than sitting."[158]

Certainly, this doesn't mean you should always walk instead of sit, rather if you need a fresh perspective or new ideas, walking can help shake things up.

Similarly, movement helps to declutter the mind to make room for new ideas.

---

157 University, Stanford. "Stanford Study Finds Walking Improves Creativity". *Stanford News*. Accessed November 8 2018. https://news.stanford.edu/2014/04/24/walking-vs-sitting-042414/.
158 Ibid.

In an excerpt from his new book, NPR host Peter Sagal writes: "If I don't leave my headphones behind when I run, I wouldn't spend a single minute of my waking life free from input."[159]

We spend most of our day consuming information from phones, friends, and street rumors. Our days are spent with things that command our full attention, usually involving lots of screens. Think about how often your attention is used in a single day. Are there ever pockets of time when your mind is neither receiving stimuli nor producing response?

Sagal realized this and decided to give up headphones while running. He says running with nothing in his ears gives him a chance to rehearse the things he's too shy to say out loud and think to the beat of a constant "left-right-left-right" metronome. These speeches often release thoughts or feeling he has bottled up during the day. He explains, "every time I let off this toxic steam—rising and evaporating with the other noxious gases from my sweaty self—I can feel the tension leave my arms and legs, and my gait becomes looser and freer. I come from a long line of shoulder-hunchers, and as I rant and I run, I can feel my back straighten and my head rise."[160]

---

159 Sagal, Peter. 2018. "The Case Against Running With Headphones". *Nytimes.Com*. Accessed November 8 2018. https://www.nytimes.com/2018/10/30/well/move/peter-sagal-book-running-without-headphones.html.
160 Ibid.

Sagal adds, "Your brain is like a duvet cover. Every once in a while, it needs to be aired out."

Movement, whether it be low intensity, like walking, or high intensity, like sprinting, serves as an almost therapeutic meditation away from the physical world. There's something cathartic and human about relying on muscle memory. You're aware of everything around you but your thoughts can be far away.

Let's take this idea of movement one step further and talk about another one of my favorite ways to play—travel.

TRAVEL

We sit oldest, middle, youngest from aisle to window as usual, so my tall legs can stretch and the littlest can wink at Barcelona's night lights as we descend through the clouds. My brain unclenches after tightly gripping theorems and vocabulary words for two weeks of finals, finally relaxing. Eight hours later, the wheels hit. My heart pounds with the rumbling of the plane, excited to spend ten days traveling three cities with fourteen family members.

In Barcelona, we tour the sites. Parque Güell, Montserrat, Toledo—traveling in time to walk through their history. We see peaceful but irate protestors demand Catalonia's independence from Spain to reclaim their autonomy. From Gaudi's Sagrada Familia, we learn to appreciate a work in progress, because there is beauty in the unfinished.

In Lisbon, we stand in line to eat centuries' old pastries made in a "Secret Shop" where they lock away the secret, actually patented, recipe. The houses are decorated with tiles—with nature and organic themes from Catholic influence and colorful patterns from Muslim influence. The mosaic assortment of the two reflect political turbulence as the city shifted from Muslim to Catholic rule.

The orange trees in Sevilla line the streets, the fruit sparkling like stars. Children flock to Christmas markets in bundled clothing and high spirits. Everyone buys grapes because at midnight you eat twelve grapes for good luck in the New Year.

When we travel, we observe. We enter a new place, perhaps unfamiliar, and commit to the process of discovery. Traveling to three cities taught me about complex history and politics, nuanced cultural traditions, and how art and religion intertwine.

Most of us know the typical travel story arch, as belabored by all study abroad-goers:

I had never traveled before, so I had no idea what to expect. I arrived, had a culture shock, and learned to immerse myself in the unfamiliar. Then I came back a different person.

The main benefit you think of when you think of travel is self-discovery, how travel humbles you and helps you reflect on your place in the world. This is important, of course, but it's not novel for most of us. The kind of travel I want to highlight in this section is one that focuses on developing empathy for strangers and noticing small problems you, in your unique position, can solve.

Travel exposes you to differences and makes you more open-minded. Jonah Lehrer, author of *Imagine*, says, "The experience of another culture endows the traveler with valuable open-mindedness, making it easier for him or her to realize that a single thing can have multiple meanings."[161]

So, when you travel, the world becomes smaller and larger. You learn to appreciate the breadth of humanity and the similarities between all people. Narrow-mindedness can't survive that.

---

161 Rohan, Lysha. "How Travel Makes You More Creative | Travel Helps Creativity". 2017. *Nomads - Discover Different*. Accessed November 8 2018. https://nomadsworld.com/travel-helps-creativity/.

This reminds me of the words that exist only in some languages and not others, to describe feelings and phenomena that are valued more heavily by certain cultures than others. In Hindi, for example, certain words just cannot be translated to English. The word *dharma* is one of them. Roughly translated to duty, *dharma* refers to the feeling of responsibility we have to fulfill all of our various roles. Regardless of how hard I try to explain it here, you likely won't grasp the full weight of the word, simply because you're unfamiliar with Indian culture. Once you take steps to understand, however, you get unique insight into a new market for which to innovate solutions.

Travel humbles you and forces you to recognize your humanity.

The wind slaps me. Its cold breath pinches my cheeks and freezes my fingers to popsicles, and I wish I bought that bright green four-leaf-clover scarf from the old lady on the street. I look down at the muddy grass, wiggling my toes in my boots to keep them warm and to make sure they're still there. The ground slopes upward, meeting the clouds on the horizon, so I trudge forward.

Head down, walk up, up, up until suddenly, grey sunlight seeps through the clouds, casting an ethereal glow across the mountain landscape. I'm almost at the top—that moment on the rollercoaster at the top, where you stretch your neck to glimpse down at the fall that comes next—and I pause.

Cliffs. I step on the crumbly part and peek over the edge, hesitant, like a kid checking for monsters under her bed, and find a ninety-degree angle. I follow the rocky edge down to where it meets the water, waves crashing in white foam explosions. I look up and out to the ocean, my eyes widening to chase where it ends. I sit on the crumbly edge of the cliffs, feet dangling, and I suddenly feel so small, so fragile. The vastness of my surrounding envelops me, squeezing me into insignificance. In this moment, nature is so much more powerful than I am.

The Cliffs of Moher are sea cliffs located on the coast of Ireland. Stretching for eight kilometers along the Atlantic coast of Clare, the cliffs reach a maximum height of 214 meters at Knockardakin. I visited the Cliffs this past October, expecting to simply visit a pretty sight. Instead, I left astounded by the sheer force of nature and feeling more human than ever.

I once read about a phenomenon that, I think, describes what I experienced: The Sublime. First coined by philosopher Edmund Burke, "The passion caused by the great and sublime in nature…is astonishment; and astonishment is that state of the soul, in which all its motions are suspended, with some degree of horror. In this case the mind is so entirely filled with its object that it cannot entertain any other."[162]

In other words, the sublime refers to the feeling you get when you're confronted with the incomprehensible magnitude of nature. It's an ineffable experience that utterly consumes you, perhaps moving you to tears, giving you a humbling sense of wonder and appreciation for the majesty of the natural world.

Traveling, whether it be to the Cliffs of Moher in Ireland, the Moki Dugway in Utah, or the mountains of Shenandoah, often nudges us in the direction of experiencing the sublime. Even if your travel involves simply going to see live music or touring an ancient library, really appreciating the beauty around you does powerful things for your perspective, and honestly, your happiness.

Travel makes you more creative and uses new parts of your brain. Travel exposes you to new people, cultures, religions, languages, and places. This exposure enables you to see more of the world and therefore more points of improvement. Innovation can be broken down into two parts: noticing inefficiencies and acting to improve them. Travel facilitates the former.

---

162 "The Sublime". 2018. *Webpages.Uidaho.Edu*. Accessed November 8 2018. https://www.webpages.uidaho.edu/engl_258/Lecture%20Notes/ sublime.htm.

According to Adam Galinsky, a Columbia business school professor who has extensively studied the link between travel and creativity, "Foreign experiences increase both cognitive flexibility and depth of thought, the ability to make deep connections between disparate forms."[163]

This is partly because travel allows us to break the everyday habits that stifle our creativity. Developmental psychologists talk about adults having learned to "dampen down" most areas of their brains so they can focus on one thing. Kids, on the other hand, don't yet do that and instead respond to multiple stimuli at once, becoming enthralled by everything around them.[164]

Spending time in different environments actually fires unused neural networks, ones that don't get used when you commute your usual path to work. The areas of the brain that adults have suppressed now become saturated with neuro-chemicals, much like a kid's brain.[165]

***

163 Crane, Brent. 2015. "For A More Creative Brain, Travel". *The Atlantic*. Accessed November 8 2018. https://www.theatlantic.com/health/ archive/2015/03/for-a-more-creative-brain-travel/388135/.
164 2018. *Creativityworkshop.Com*. Accessed November 8 2018. https:// creativityworkshop.com/articles/travelandcreativity.
165 Ibid.

On the field is about engaging in activities intended for play and capitalizing on their creative and learning potential. Whether you learn mental toughness from sports, break down complex violin concerto into single notes, or let nature overwhelm you through travel, going out on the field during recess time has innumerable benefits.

CHAPTER 9

SANDCASTLES

———

"I have put so much more into this house than you or any other client has a right to expect, that if I don't have your confidence—to hell with the whole thing," Frank Lloyd Wright said to his client, Edgar Kaufman, about the house he was designing.[166]

Kaufman wanted a house with a view of the Bear Run stream falls in western Pennsylvania. Wright designed a house that sat atop the falls, peeking out of the hills just enough to disappear into the scenery, blurring that line between man-made structure and nature itself. Wright's bold design

---

166 Glancey, Jonathan. 2001. "The Folly Of Fallingwater". *The Guardian*. Accessed November 8 2018. https://www.theguardian.com/culture/2001/sep/10/artsfeatures.

and unwavering, perhaps dangerously so, self-conviction impressed Kaufman enough to earn a green light.

Fallingwater was a breathtaking sight but a structural nightmare. When construction began in 1936, Kaufman brought in consulting engineers to double check the design. Even though Wright was too proud to heed to the engineers' requests, the engineers added additional reinforcing steel to support the beams holding the living room up.

Even with the added beams, by the time the house was finished in 1939, the ceiling was already sagging. By 1995, the ceiling was sagging from a maximum of nine feet to a dangerously low six feet four inches. As a result of the stressed concrete and sagging ceiling, engineers rushed to fix the beams that hold the house up. They added an entire secondary structural system to relieve and distribute the stresses on the old beams.

Fallingwater was falling down. It was a miracle it had lasted as long as it had, and that's mostly because those sneaky engineers acted on their foresight. As beautiful as the home was, the structure wasn't properly designed to evenly distribute the weight.[167]

---

167 Ibid.

Wright's old colleague, Louis Sullivan, came up with the much-quoted principle: "Form forever follows function."

In other words, the primary purpose of something is what it does; its appearance can only be a result of that function. Things are only as good as the structure upon which they are built. For buildings, that means evenly distributing the weight so the ceiling doesn't collapse.

Turns out that play can help with reinforcement and stability. You can play in ways that distribute the weight of various pressures placed on you.

***

Sandcastles: Diversification. It means diversifying the things you build and how you build them.

You're always building something, whether you know it or not. An academic career, company mission, physical strength, cooking skills, personal wealth, and the list goes on.

Sandcastles encourages you to build more and build better. Using free time to build not only turns out to give you more options but also is usually really fulfilling.

If you don't diversify and distribute, you may not hit a glass ceiling, but you'll hit a sinking ceiling.

＊

As I was typing this chapter on the train to DC, I started talking to my neighbor and his three-and-a-half-year-old son. When I asked him what he does, he first said he worked for the State Department. He didn't smile. I began to put together a semi-excited response when he interrupted, "But I run a foreign language school on the side."

He smiled.

He used to be a food writer and always had a passion for learning about different cultures. His work at the State Department "is a lot of paperwork. It's fine, but it's—"

"—not really fulfilling, right?" I interjected.

"Exactly."

He divides his time between the three things—job, school, kid—time-managing meticulously so as to not shaft any one priority.

"There's lots you can get done when you don't use Facebook and don't repeat yourself."

He then proceeded to market his various foreign language offerings and international immersion trips to me and my sister, and we politely offered to help him put up fliers in our school.

Many people are unfulfilled. Building little things, anything from small passion projects to real estate empires, is a good solution to a common problem.

WHAT ARE YOU BUILDING?

In an earlier chapter, "Digging for Worms," we discussed the use of design thinking to move the scientific method from the lab to the mind. This allows you to analyze your needs, empathize with yourself, and ideate and prototype in order to achieve your dream life.

What are you building right now? An academic career? A professional career? Physical fitness? Patience? Tolerance?

Take a minute to think about your day, and divide your hours based on *what you're building*.

Today, mine (skipping meals) looked something like this:

9 a.m. – 10 a.m.: **Mental Health** (Meditation and Yoga)

10 a.m. – 12:30 p.m.: **Passion Project** (Book)

2 p.m. – 3 p.m.: **Physical Fitness** (Running)

3 p.m. – 6 p.m.: **Academic Career** (Homework)

6 p.m.-8 p.m.: **Passion Project** (Book)

9 p.m. – 11 p.m.: **Family Relationships** (Movie with sisters)

Thankfully I'm writing this on a Sunday at home during a long weekend from school. If this was during a time when I had a full-time job/internship, the day would look more like:

9 a.m. – 6 p.m.: **Company Mission** (Work)

6 p.m. – 8 p.m.: **Friendships** (Out to Dinner)

8 p.m. – 10 p.m.: **Netflix's Revenue** (watch Netflix)

10 p.m.: **My Dreams** (Sleep)

Most people have something they want to do but are not doing. I have very entrepreneurial friends who read Crunchbase and TechNews and talk about Elon Musk but keep pushing off their potential side hustles to opt for more "predictable" success.

Their experiences in other sectors, with more "security and stability" may help them gain skills, connections, and exposure. They may also make them more, as Andrew Yang says, "socialized and specialized, more risk averse, and accustomed to operating in resource-rich environments with a narrow set of deliverables."[168]

They begin to lose a sense of personal identity because original thinking isn't in their job description. When people only build one thing, they're creating a single story and a single source of credibility. They endanger themselves by putting too much pressure on one beam, resulting in not only a lack of individuality but also financial instability that comes with only one source of income.

Inc magazine sat down with Elon Musk to talk about this danger, this structural weakness, that comes with focusing too much on a college degree.

"If somebody graduated from a great university that may be an indication that they will be capable of great things, but it's not necessarily the case. If you look at people like Bill Gates and Steve Jobs... if you could hire them, you would."[169]

Bryan Caplan, George Mason University Economist, suggests that there are two dominant schools of thought on the returns to education. The traditional view is that college

---

168 Yang, Andrew. 2014. *Smart People Should Build Things*.

169 Stillman, Jessica. 2018. "Elon Musk To The Young And Ambitious: Skills Matter More Than Degrees". 2017. *Inc.Com*. Accessed November 8 2018. https://www.inc.com/jessica-stillman/why-elon-musk-doesnt-care-about-college-degrees.html.

builds human capital, equipping students with the skills they need to succeed in life beyond. The other view derives from game theory and holds that graduating college is just an elaborate signaling effect, a simple mark of credibility to employers that college grads have what it takes to succeed.[170]

I find this extremely funny because I go to college and know what happens here. We sit in lectures, some of us pay attention and most of us do not. We con our way through easy classes and retain very little information, simply because we don't need to learn to boost our GPA. Since half the things we do are in pursuit of a job, we seldom learn for the sake of learning or build real skills.

I actually just showed you the power of the signaling effect; in fact, I have done it multiple times in this book. When I introduce people, to prove their credibility, I mention what school they are affiliated with. How else am I meant to convince you the source is credible? I want you to evaluate Caplan's work, but I worry that you won't even get that far if he doesn't have the title to support it.

Caplan also brings up the "sheepskin effect." This is the well-known fact that the returns to a college education do not

---

170 "College: Capital Or Signal? | Economic Man". 2018. *Economicman-blog.Com*. Accessed November 8 2018. http://www.economicmanblog.com/college-capital-or-signal/.

accrue evenly over the four years. Approximately 70 percent of the earnings increase comes from getting the diploma that last year, a fact inconsistent with the linear model implied by the human capital theory.[171]

Musk, instead of buying into the signaling effect of a college degree, talks about building skills, "Look for evidence of exceptional ability, and if there's a track record of exceptional achievement then it's likely that will continue into the future."[172]

When high school students cater their whole lives in hopes to get admitted into a single college, and when college students do the same for a single job, they invest 100 percent of their time in the prospects of obtaining something they don't even know if they'll enjoy. According to a Gallup poll, approximately 51 percent of college students regret one of their college education choices. Similarly, according to a 2017 Gallup poll, 70 percent of American workers are not engaged in their work.[173] In 2013, *Forbes* reported that "work is more

---

171 Ibid.

172 Stillman, Jessica. 2018. "Elon Musk To The Young And Ambitious: Skills Matter More Than Degrees". 2017. *Inc.Com*. Accessed November 8 2018. https://www.inc.com/jessica-stillman/why-elon-musk-doesnt-care-about-college-degrees.html.

173 Gallup, Inc. 2017. "Do You Regret Your College Choices?". *Gallup.Com*. Accessed November 8 2018. https://news.gallup.com/opinion/gallup/211070/regret-college-choices.aspx.

often a source of frustration than fulfillment for 90 percent of the world's workers." [174]

When you focus on only one goal, you make yourself vulnerable to total collapse.

So, how do we go about diversifying what we build?

We have to look at how we spend our time now and honestly see how we currently invest our time. We have to treat time like any other investment.

Time Value of Time

Congratulations? You just won a surprise cash prize from a raffle you entered for some reason! You can either receive your money, say $500,000 now, or in three years. What do you do?

If you know the time value of money, you know where this is going, so skip a bit. Most people would take the money now because they know that in three years that $500,000 will be worth less. And that's true. But taking the money now

174 Adams, Susan. 2018. "Unhappy Employees Outnumber Happy Ones By Two To One Worldwide". *Forbes*. Accessed November 8 2018. https://www.forbes.com/sites/susanadams/2013/10/10/unhappy-employees-outnumber-happy-ones-by-two-to-one-worldwide/#630bf-73c362a.

gives you the opportunity to increase the future value of your money by investing and gaining interest over a period of time. The timeline below[175] shows this:

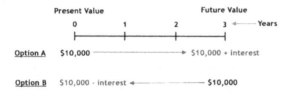

Given the money you have today, depending on what you do with it, you have the opportunity to grow it to make it worth more at a future time.

Seems pretty obvious, and most people do know this about money. Some people even take this knowledge and do something about it. What most people don't know is that there is a value of time itself as well. A second, minute, or hour today is worth more than its tomorrow counterpart.

An interactive visualization done by Australian Designer Maximilian Kiener (highly recommend you look it up) illustrates how our relationships with time changes as we grow older.

---

175 Carther, Shauna. 2003. "Understanding The Time Value Of Money". *Investopedia*. Accessed November 8 2018. https://www.investopedia. com/articles/03/082703.asp.

When you're one year old, one year is all the time you've ever known. That year is, quite literally, your forever. When you're two, a year is half of your whole life. When you're nineteen, a year is 5.6 percent of your life. "Your summer vacation in your first year in college will feel like your whole seventy-sixth year."[176]

As you grow older and older, one year is a smaller and smaller fraction of your life. Paul Janet, a French philosopher, first proposed the idea of time perception in 1897. While not a universally accepted theory, it does propose some implications worth thinking about—the main one being that we perceive time by comparing it with our life span. The apparent length of a period of time is proportional to our life span itself.

In other terms, my favorite terms (mathematical terms), our perception of time is logarithmic, where the year is on the x axis and our perception of the speed of that year is represented by the slope of the line.[177]

The bottom line here is that your time now is worth more than your time in the future. People always think that some way somehow they will have time eventually to do the thing

---

176 Kiener, Maximilian. 2018. "Why Time Flies". *Maximiliankiener.Com.* Accessed November 8 2018. https://www.maximiliankiener.com/digitalprojects/time/.
177 Ibid.

they dream of doing. But our perception of time only speeds up as time passes.

Truth is, time, like money, needs to be budgeted and invested intentionally to recognize the time-value of time.

INVEST TIME LIKE MONEY

Robert Kiyosaki, author of *Rich Dad Poor Dad* and self-made businessman, offers a particularly helpful model to illustrate what it means to "think like an investor."

In his book, *The Business of the 21st Century,* Kiyosaki shares his Cashflow Quadrant.[178] The quadrant is a table divided into four areas, much like any Cartesian graph with four quadrants.

According to Kiyosaki, the business world is made of these four different people. Even though people can be in more than one quadrant, they often spend most of their time in just one.

- **E= Employee**: You work for a company and have linear income (i.e., you trade your time for money). In order to make more money, you must work more hours. Or, you can switch to

---

178 Kiyosaki, Robert T, John Fleming, and Kim Kiyosaki. 2013. *The Business Of The 21St Century*. Lake Dallas, Tex.: Success Partners.

a higher-paying job. You focus on getting a "safe, secure job with benefits."

- **S= Self-Employed**: You are a small-business owner who believes that if you want something done right, you have to do it by yourself. Generally, a one-person act, perhaps a doctor with your own practice, you enjoy a bit more personal freedom than employees, but you are still required to trade your time for money.

- **B= Business Owner**: You have a big business with five hundred or more employees. You want to create a sound business based on a good system, good network, and smart people. You "want smart people to run the company," and receive passive income from ownership (i.e., you don't have to be working for the business to generate income).

- **I= Investor**: You truly have passive income. You have built more than one self-generating income asset (i.e., stocks, bonds, real estate, businesses, copyrights, royalties...etc.) and enjoy the benefits of financial and personal freedom. You live in retirement because you let the money work for you.[179]

You can to shift from a linear way of using your time to an exponential one by migrating to the I quadrant. Go back to the list of the things you are currently building with your time. Are you operating in the E quadrant, building one thing only? Or are you building several different assets?

---

179 Ibid.

For my finance bros, I think of time and building diversification as achieving optimal asset allocation. According to Investopedia, diversification in finance means that "a portfolio constructed of different kinds of investments will, on average, yield higher returns and pose a lower risk than any individual investment found within the portfolio...it strives to smooth out unsystematic risk events in a portfolio so the positive performance of some investments neutralizes the negative performance of others."[180]

Asset allocation is the strategy of dividing your investment portfolios across various asset classes, like stocks, bonds, and money market securities. The main goal of allocating your assets is to maximize return while minimizing risk. Every asset has a different risk-return tradeoff (i.e., equities have the highest potential return, but also the highest risk. Treasury bills, on the other hand, have the lowest risk and lowest return).

Since different asset classes have different risk-return tradeoffs, diversification through asset allocation is important. Asset allocation insulates your entire portfolio from the fluctuations of a single class of securities.

---

180 Gustafson, Bob. 2015. "Portfolio Rebalancing - Balancing Risk And Return". *Triton Financial Group.* Accessed November 8 2018. https://tritonfinancialgroup.com/portfolio-rebalancing/.

So, what are assets and how do we build them?

Assets are:

- Business or Side Hustles You Build Yourself
- Transferable Skill Sets You Teach Yourself
- Passive Learning Through Secondary Building

Financial income and human capital income are the single two most important ways of achieving security and stability in our lives. We'll go through each of these asset groups so you can see just how many ways there are to make passive income, diversify, and build sandcastles.

BUILDING A SKILL SET

The peppered moth used to be a light color with black spots. During the Industrial Revolution, as the London air filled with soot and the light colored trees became darker. The birds started to eat the light colored months more readily. Within months, the moths became darker and lighter moths were rare. After the Industrial Revolution, light colored moths were once again found in greater numbers.

Natural selection is the "process whereby organisms better adapted to their environment tend to survive and produce offspring."[181] Essentially, it's the idea that nature favors certain traits, and those who have those traits have a higher fitness, or ability to survive and reproduce to create fertile offspring. AKA, the winning genes survive and reproduce over generations to create a winning species.

What makes some species more likely to survive than others? In a constantly changing and unpredictable environment, anything can happen to select against or for any given trait.

The answer? Genetic Variation.

Variation exists within species already. Some individuals are taller, faster, more colorful, or smarter than others. The environment favors certain traits over others, so those with those traits have a higher likelihood of survival than those without them. From an overall population level, genetic variation is extremely important; the more homogeneous a species is, the higher likelihood it can be wiped out by an unpredictable natural force.

Building skillsets is a way to increase your fitness. The more variation you have in your toolkit, the better prepared you

181 "Genetic Variation And Natural Selection: Natural Selection". 2018. *Infoplease*. Accessed November 8 2018. https://www.infoplease.com/science/biology/genetic-variation-and-natural-selection-natural-selection.

are to react to unpredictable situations. While there are lots of ways to intentionally develop skills and exposure, I focus on the one I find most important—reading.

Charlie Munger once said, "In my whole life, I have known no wise people (over a broad subject matter area) who didn't read all the time—none. Zero."[182]

The busiest people in the world make time for reading, and rightfully so. I mean Bill Gates can read a book a week... and he's Bill *Gates*.

Why does he do that? Because he knows the more he knows and learns, the better equipped he is at adapting to his environment. He agrees with Benjamin Franklin when he said, "An investment in knowledge pays the best interest."

Our environment right now selects people who are constantly learning; those who work hard but don't take the time to learn new skills will "be the new "at-risk" group. They risk losing their jobs to automation, just like workers

---

182 Simmons, Michael. 2017. "5-Hour Rule: If You'Re Not Spending 5 Hours Per Week Learning, You'Re Being Irresponsible". 2017. *Medium*. Accessed November 8 2018. https://medium.com/the-mission/the-5-hour-rule-if-youre-not-spending-5-hours-per-week-learning-you-re-being-irresponsible-791c3f18f5e6.

did when robots replace 85 percent of manufacturing jobs between 2000 and 2010.[183]

The people at the top with the most skills are getting compensated more than ever, and the people at the bottom are losing their jobs to robots.

In order to survive in this environment, you need to master, as some call it, the "new knowledge economy."[184] You can do this by creating your own learning plan. Find time to learn something, regardless of how busy you are. Once you find that time, treat it like a responsibility and hold yourself accountable.

In short, surviving today requires constantly learning new things and developing new skills. So, use the internet to your advantage, and do it!

SECONDARY BUILDING

I walk into Tower 49, the 360 elevator mirror delivering on its 9 a.m. promise to remind me just how my hair frizzes in exactly the wrong way after a twenty-block walk through a Manhattan summer morning. The elevator is

---

183 Ibid.
184 Ibid.

sardine-packed with "comfy-casual" business hippies replacing business cards with laptop stickers and claustrophobic cubicles with Beanbag chairs.

I get to floor six. Bright yellow orbs dangle from the ceiling and glass walls partition the open space, replacing the dizzying fluorescent lights so familiar in the traditional office setting. Flat-screen TVs and over-the-door basketball hoops pepper the halls, coloring the workday with childlike energy. People walk around, free to take coffee breaks or play shuffleboard or watch the World Cup on the big screen, at WeWork, we build on our own time.

This past summer, I worked for a real estate technology startup, Landis Technologies Inc. I wrote earlier about how I was hired, but essentially I had no real estate experience beyond watching *Million Dollar Listing* on TV and inspecting country town homes on Sotheby's website. Using some playground principles like monkey bars and slide, I jumped right into a whole new world so I could add value and help them build.

Over the course of ten weeks, I helped the two cofounders build their vision of the largest online B2B marketplace for single family rental homes. As their first hire and only business development employee on the team, I worked in all aspects of the company. Mostly, I analyzed and optimized outreach methods, proposed broader company strategy suggestions, and managed relationships with both billionaire investors and mom-and-pop house flippers.

In the process of helping them build, I developed skills in sales, marketing, and strategy, among others. In contrast to intentionally setting out to develop sales skills by reading a book or registering for a course, I developed different skillsets inadvertently in pursuit of something bigger. I also learned about hiring, negotiation, industry-specific culture, and other intangible assets I was privy to because of my position as a secondary builder.

Secondary building is a great way to learn things that become transferrable elsewhere. It requires working close to a project that is being built, instead of spearheading it. Some ways to build secondarily include:

1. Interviewing someone who is building or has built something interesting
2. Consulting on a project you're not totally familiar with
3. Editing essays or work for others in new subjects
4. Working for a Startup
5. And more...

I am biased to working for a startup, mainly because my experience was so transformative and helpful in equipping me with skillsets and insights I wouldn't have otherwise had.

As Startup Institute co-founder Aaron O'Hearn puts it, "Startup employees rarely work within the confines of one job description. You have to be willing to roll up your sleeves and get your hands dirty in a lot of different facets of the business."[185]

Working for a startup allows you to diversify what you do and what you learn without necessarily having the risk of building your own business.

BUILD SOMETHING YOURSELF

Whether it's a business, a YouTube channel, or a novel, working on an ongoing passion project is the primary way to build sandcastles.

My neighbor has a side hustle where he does custom henna tattoos for people on campus. Posting his designs on Instagram and receiving positive feedback reminds him of his gifted talent.

---

185 "4 Unexpected Ways A Startup Can Accelerate Your Career". 2015. *Themuse.Com*. Accessed November 8 2018. https://www.themuse.com/advice/4-unexpected-ways-a-startup-can-accelerate-your-career.

My sister, Ritika, spends her evenings writing and recording songs. When I left for college, she transformed my bedroom into a music studio. She released her first single, "Wrong Expectations" October 2018 (shameless plug—go listen on Spotify, Apple Music, or YouTube!)

My sister, Tarika, does art in her free time. When she's not sketching in her textbook, her eye is pressed against the lens of her camera, filming amateur documentaries or video scrapbooks of our travel adventures. She shares her perspective through what she creates.

My parents, Shivaram and Anjali Kumar, replaced their linear income decades ago by building a successful network marketing business—a debt-free business asset that has enabled them with unparalleled financial and personal freedom. So much freedom that they often ask my sisters and I to skip school to travel with them. I'm so lucky and grateful that they build sandcastles the way they do.

I'm working on an app, writing a book, developing a podcast, and making my own college major. Building all of these things injects my life with purpose and autonomy. I'm trying to build within every structure I'm a part of, which is supposed to help my day be dominated by building. Some days it is. Some days it isn't. I can't wait for when I get to spend my whole day building.

None of these examples are motivated primarily by financial gain although that can provide a compelling reason to start a side hustle. The bigger point here is that engaging in these side activities dramatically benefits the person doing them.

These are my reasons for starting a side hustle:

1. Gain Autonomy—when you start to work on something you take ownership of, you get to decide your strategy. Working for a boss at a job or a professor in class means you're not setting the rubric you're being judged with. A side project lets you call the shots, and, in doing so, gives you more confidence.
2. Develop Skills—you learn a lot by doing, especially if you are doing something you've never done before. I learned more about starting a business through writing this book than through my introduction to entrepreneurship class.
3. Relieve Stress and Boredom—when you do things you don't want to do, you can become frustrated with the fact that your actions don't match your desires. It can be really stressful when all your hours are spent doing something you don't enjoy.
4. Burst the Bubble—a side hustle lets you operate in different roles simultaneously. When we have one focus, we can tend to isolate ourselves within that bubble. Building something outside the bubble allows us to zoom out to the big picture and build new relationships.
5. Potential Financial Opportunities— side hustles let you diversify your income and get closer to financial freedom.

Side hustles are businesses, hobbies, platforms, blogs, skill-sets, and essentially anything else that generates some kind of financial and human capital income.

***

I often think back to my visit to Alberobello, a small town in Puglia, Italy, to visualize this idea.

Alberobello has been made a UNESCO World Heritage Site for its unusual districts of *trulli*, these characteristic white-washed conical-roofed houses that line the streets of the town. (Google it!) Alberobello was originally designed to evade taxes and fool the authorities. Count Acuaviva, the local feudal lord, moved his peasant workers there to cultivate the land. To wiggle around the laws, he had to ensure Alberobello didn't qualify as an inhabited settlement. So, the *trulli*, where people lived, were specifically designed so they could be dismantled in a hurry when the authorities arrived.[186]

The name, *trullo*, comes from the Greek word for *dome*, τρούλος (in Italian, cupola). *Trulli* are simple and small dwellings constructed out of local limestone. The thickness of the walls and the lack of windows regulate the internal

---

186 "Alberobello Tourist Information | Italy Heaven". 2018. *Italyheaven. Co.Uk.* Accessed November 8 2018. http://www.italyheaven.co.uk/puglia/alberobello.html.

temperature of the house so that it stays warm in the winter and cool in the summer. The roof is a dome-like structure made of limestone positioned in series of diminishing concentric circles, called *chianche* and *chiancarelle*.[187] All the stones that comprise the roof look the same, except for a single one known as the keystone. They keystone is the most important structural element of the house; if you pull it out, the whole structure falls apart.

These houses have everything going for them. They even have thermal equilibrium. But the houses, however stable they may seem, are built around one point of weakness.

Sandcastles are about diversifying assets to distribute structural pressure and build skills that lead to security and fulfillment. Do this by building a business or a skillset individually or by proximity. Diversifying your time and assets will safeguard you both against structural weaknesses and boredom.

Building sandcastles is my favorite way to play because it is how we catapult ourselves into designing the lifestyle we want.

---

187 Ibid.

SCHOOL'S OUT

——

A FINAL REFLECTION

I see hopscotch as my feet hit the pavement—one, two, one, two, one, two—setting a metronome for my diverse playlist of country jams and Bollywood tunes. Crunchy brown leaves form whipped cream dollops on my left, tempting me to jump and sink into the fluff. On my right, the golden-hour warmth lights up the robot rowers on the Potomac in an orange flame floating down the river. My arms swing back and forth and the cold wind turns my fingers into snow-capped mountains, but I run for the fresh air so I can't complain.

I make it to the monuments and skip to the top of the Lincoln Memorial, my feet dangling off the top step. I look down at the flocks of tourists pass by, with their selfie sticks and neon visors, and smile when their eyes widen at first sight of the Washington Monument. I glance around until I notice the kids on my left, sliding down the side of the Lincoln Memorial. They slide down, taking turns with other kids they don't know. One girl struggles to climb back up so another kid grabs her arm and helps her up. Adults look over with "FOMO," and I refuse to become like them.

Nervous, but remembering my recently-edited *Monkey Bars* and *Slide* chapters, I tell myself to go play. Practice what I write about and just do it. So, I do. And it feels amazing. I slide down, kicking my feet in the air and conceding my fate to gravity. An adrenaline pulse runs through my veins, and for a moment I forget everything. Giddy, I climb up and go down again.

Liberated.

HOW I'VE CHANGED

The process of writing this book has truly added a layer of play to my life. Everywhere I go, I look for playground principles. I keep an eye out for pirates that creep into my mind in bored moments, and I let my daydreams stumble upon innovations. I bring a box of crayons with me to every meeting or group project, ready to color outside the lines to find creative solutions. I let go and grab monkey bars with less hesitation, less prevention, and more promotion.

Take what happened in my Foundations of Entrepreneurship class (if you can even call it that) the other day, for example.

Glasses on, hair curly, and sweatpant groutfit, I dragged my feet to class Monday morning after an all-nighter writing this book. This was all-nighter number eight of what became approximately 20 all-nighters of intense writing, editing, and revising this book before launch. I talked to nobody except google scholar and my mom, often in tears because I wasn't sure I'd pull this off in time. I pretended like I had no other work and tunnel-vision focused on my book and only my book until it was done.

So, needless to say, I did not read the case we were supposed to read for class. I walked into the room 15 minutes late with eyes barely open and hot coffee dripping off my chin, looking like a homeless person who spent the night on a bench outside the library. Truly a tragic aesthetic. In any case, I was in that beyond-tired-giggly mood, so as soon as we broke out into discussion groups, I started goofing around and laughing.

"So, who wants to sell me this scooter?" My professor grins at us, squinting his eyes in search of a target.

I laugh louder than I listen, and I accidentally make eye contact with my professor. Whoops.

"Devika, you seem to be in a good mood today. Why don't you come up here and sell me this scooter?"

Alright. Guess I'm doing this now.

"Sure!"

And then, I sold him a scooter. I whipped out some cold-calling techniques I had practiced at my internship over the summer, some "Happy Friday!" and "Did you catch the Arsenal game last night?" I got him to talk about himself and identify his two pain-points he hopes a new scooter will fix. Even though I had no idea what our scooter looked like, what it offered, or how much it cost, I played a game of improvisation, because I really had nothing to lose. And it worked.

Because I am now committed to digging for worms and experimentation, I was not attached to outcomes. Instead, I was rapidly ideating on the spot, which turned out to both be really fun and result in a successful sale. Jumping into a task (Monkey Bars) and figuring out what I could do on the fly expanded my RDF (Pirates on Lava) and helped me realize I can do more than I think. Looking stupid in front of my peers may have scared me in the past, because school stigmatizes mistakes and rewards perfection, but it didn't even cross my mind that day. My intention was to simply have fun and see what I could do.

Playing is so liberating, and all it really involves is a bit of intentionality about your perspective. If you see the world as your playground, opportunities to play present themselves to you all over the place.

Since I adopted a playground perspective, I have done some truly amazing and rewarding things. I embraced tag and travel when my neighbor spontaneously asked me to skip school and go to Dublin with him and his friends one weekend and I said yes. On that trip, I became more independent by exploring a new place and getting to know new people. I felt like I had the capacity to be adventurous and spontaneous, and I'm grateful for my book because it helped me foresee the power that a weak tie could have on my personal development.

Writing the sandcastles chapter was an inception-like experience, because my book has been my sandcastle for a whole year now. When piecing together this book, I was discovering new things all the time. I developed theories, tested things, experimented with organization and structure, and searched the corners of the internet for unique stories to tell. I called up strangers to interview them for the book and refined my inner circle with like-minded people who could give me companionship in my ambition.

My book has been a framework that has permeated my life in all aspects. Most importantly, this project has infused a sense of purpose into my every day, something that college truly neglects. In subscribing to a semester schedule in which everything I do for a few months suddenly evaporates at the start of a new semester, I felt like my work didn't matter. I felt like I wasn't learning anything or building skills, because I could just forget after an exam.

This book, this tangible creation, broke the cycle of impermanence in education. It empowered me to play through my boredom instead of complain about it. It allowed me to learn on my own time through hands-on creation. The book showed me problems with the education system and presented solutions to them.

EDUCATION REFORM

Throughout the book, I have hinted at ways schools can improve to integrate play to promote better learning, creativity, and happiness. I have talked about the factory-like model schools adopt to output homogeneity. I have also talked about the pipeline problem of pigeonholing students earlier and earlier on, forcing them to decide their long-term fate too soon. You also read about, perhaps in every chapter, how schools squander the talent, resilience, and creativity we have as kids.

I love this anecdote from Ken Robinson's Ted Talk, so I printed it below for you[188].

I heard a great story recently -- I love telling it -- of a little girl who was in a drawing lesson. She was six, and she was at the back, drawing, and the teacher said this girl hardly ever paid attention, and in this drawing lesson, she did. The teacher was fascinated. She went over to her, and she said, "What are you drawing?" And the girl said, "I'm drawing a picture of God." And the teacher said, "But nobody knows what God looks like." And the girl said, "They will, in a minute."

What these things have in common is that kids will take a chance. If they don't know, they'll have a go. Am I right? They're not frightened of being wrong. I don't mean to say that being wrong is the same thing as being creative. What we do know is, if you're not prepared to be wrong, you'll never come up with anything original -- if you're not prepared to be wrong. And by the time they get to be adults, most kids have lost that capacity. They have become frightened of being wrong. And we run

188 Robinson, Ken. 2018. "Do Schools Kill Creativity?". *Ted.Com.* Accessed November 21 2018. https://www.ted.com/talks/ ken_robinson_says_schools_kill_creativity?language=en.

our companies like this. We stigmatize mistakes. And we're now running national education systems where mistakes are the worst thing you can make. And the result is that we are educating people out of their creative capacities.[189]

If you think of it, the whole system of public education around the world is a protracted process of university entrance. And the consequence is that many highly-talented, brilliant, creative people think they're not, because the thing they were good at school wasn't valued, or was actually stigmatized. And I think we can't afford to go on that way.

The good thing is, there are many opportunities for growth and change. The one I advocate for most is student ownership and making a choice to become a trailblazer and personalize your own education. This solution really involves doing two things:

1. Create recess time beyond the 9-5 to enrich your personal education
2. Embody playground principles to integrate play into your overall perspective of the world

The onus is on the individual to game their way out of boredom, and I hope this booked help inspire you to play, create, and live a little more like a kid.

---

189 Ibid.

Schools themselves have a long way to go. The following quote said by Dolores Umbridge in Harry Potter and the Order of the Phoenix (best book, we can talk about it) sums it up well:

"It is the view of the Ministry that a theoretical knowledge will be sufficient to get you through your examinations, which after all, is what school is all about."

Schools need to change to prioritize learning over performance. A good way to do that is to create a collaborative environment for experimentation, ideation, and play.

I talk about Pixar and IDEO so often because I think schools can learn a lot from how they operate. Structurally, their offices are deliberately designed to promote interdisciplinary collaboration and movement. Employees there are given a chance to take ownership of their space and decorate it however they like. Imagine if, when you thought of a classroom, you didn't think of students sitting in rows staring at a chalkboard.

Classrooms should have some personality and some space to collaborate. Imagine if students were given more chances to encounter subjects or people they had little experience with? Diversity — of thought, or anything else — really contributes nothing if people aren't given the change to expose themselves to that diversity. So, first suggestion to schools, reorganize the structure of the environment to promote interdisciplinary discoveries and play.

IDEO and Pixar also create a culture schools can benefit from replicating. These companies destigmatize mistakes and embrace experimentation. They are innovative places where people love to work precisely because they embody "responsible abandon" and play. Schools should shift to prioritize creation and invention, instead of memorization and performance.

While still a minority, there are some schools that have definitely begun taking steps in the right direction, like High Tech High.

Founded by former lawyer Larry Rosenstock, High Tech High is a collection of charter schools in Southern California (shocker) that focus on project-based learning (PBL).[190] PBL encourages students to learn in the process of creating and engineering inventions. At this school, students develop really interesting projects, like bilingual cookbooks. Pictures from Google indicate also that structure of the facility reflects openness and play.

---

190 "What Schools Can Learn From Google, IDEO, And Pixar". 2011. *Fast Company*. Accessed November 21 2018. https://www.fastcompany. com/1664735/what-schools-can-learn-from-google-ideo-and-pixar.

Slowly, but surely, schools and education systems will shift to prepare students for the information age, not the industrial age. It is just a matter of when.

I hope to help accelerate that change.

My next steps are to chip away at transforming education in schools and workplaces. Maybe I'll set up playgrounds for all ages, with full-sized slides and monkey bars. Maybe I'll start my own school. Maybe I'll collaborate on projects with others, perhaps some of you, to share the message and promote the benefits of play. Not sure, but excited to see how it plays (wink wink) out.

PLAY EVERYWHERE

A week before this book launched, my sister and I were standing in line for the rain home. We took an 8pm train the Monday before Thanksgiving, so the line was really long.

Arched like old-people canes leaning against a wall, everyone in line hunches over their phones as if the Apple rectangle was a crystal ball that could predict the future. The line stretches across the wingspan of Union Station, Washington DC, because for some reason people prefer to stand up and wait than sit down and wait.

"Why do we line up so early? I don't understand this. Also, why is everyone so boring?" I say to my sister, just loud enough so the people nearby could hear.

"Why is everyone on their phone, doing nothing? Let's dance."

I start dancing in line. Like, embarrassing dancing. The kind of dancing your dad does when you make the mistake of letting him pick you up from the homecoming dance. And then I start laughing. My sister starts laughing. The person standing next to me starts laughing— not *at* me, but because I'm his comedic entertainment.

"You're so right. People *are* boring," says a man in line.

The man then proceeds to unzip his backpack and pull out what looks like two halves of a jump rope with weights at the ends. He looks left and right, scanning his periphery to ensure there are no security guards around.

Then, he starts swinging them around. Across his body, over his head, through his legs.

"I'm a fire-thrower. They call me 'Hobbit.' I learned how to breathe and throw fire in Hawaii. It's called *Poi*."

Necks all rise and twist in unison to see fire-throwing, hold the fire, courtesy of Hobbit. He narrates the story of discovering his passion, learning the art of *poi*, and how play has helped him become successful in his career as a computer scientist. I tell him about my book, and he preorders it.

It only takes one person to transform a dull moment into a fun one, and I want readers of this book to be motivated to be that person. If enough people view the world like a playground, then the world becomes a playground— a place where we can eat dirt and get back up, unclench all the potential energy we store in the bottom of our gut as we get old, and hang upside down to watch the clouds become our floor and the grass become our sky, enchanted by how our entire world can flip in just one moment.

ACKNOWLEDGEMENTS

—

My gratitude for life cannot fit on a page. Below is my simple attempt to just barely scratch the surface of how grateful I am for the environment I was raised in and the people who surround me.

First thank you goes to my parents, Shivaram and Anjali Kumar. Your youthful vibrancy and joie de vivre exist in stark contrast to the monolith of average adulthood. You reassure me that it is possible to stay young and fun forever. Thank you for dreaming big enough to provide us with an unparalleled lifestyle of freedom, travel, love, and happiness. Papa, your electric energy and candid delivery draws crowds of eager listeners wherever you go. From reading all the Harry Potter books in 1 week, to publishing your own book, to producing your own movie, and to investing in projects, you inspire us with your never-ending ambition and hunger for accomplishing. Mama, your sincerity and grace elevate you to the highest level of classiness imaginable. Strangers can feel the warmth of your generosity hug them from miles away. You've taught me that people remember how you make them feel more than anything else. So, it's really no wonder why everyone always remembers you — even if they only met you for a moment.

Mama and Papa, I'm blessed to have you two as my parents, and I'm even luckier that science tells me I'll be like you when I grow up.

To my sisters, Tarika and Ritika, you are the best friends and prank-targets an older sister can have. Ritika, you are more than cute. You are a thoughtful and intelligent soul, brightening up the world with your smile and touching lives with your lyrics. Thank you for allowing me to maintain my innocence and awe alongside you growing up. Tarika, you are simply brilliant. When you teach yourself Python, complicated guitar solos, and graphic design in your free time, you also teach me how to optimize my recess time to become better. You don't chase excellence; it chases you, desperately grasping for inspiration in the dust you leave behind. Also, thank you both very much for coming to the movies in your pajamas with me and letting me embarrass you in public.

More family! Alka Mama and Jijipapa, your spontaneity takes you to explore corners of the world and inspires me to embrace adventure. Thank you to Arjun and Viresh and all my cousins, aunts, uncles, and grandparents for emulating successful, loving relationships and supporting us in whatever we do.

Thank you to my business family, business conferences, and positive associations. Your lessons have made the world a better place, one where anyone with any background can seize the American Dream as long as they have the right attitude. Thank you to Kanti Uncle and Lata Fui for showing me that life is about more than fancy degrees; it's about adding value to others.

To my peers and teachers—Mr. Asch, Dr. Gadd, Mr. Rhodes, Mr. Cara, Mr. Q, Señora Kamen, Mr. Madani, Señora Simonds, Ms. Mangino, Mr. Gudgel, Coach Adams, and all the others—at Princeton Day School, thank you for challenging and encouraging me to make creative connections.. I am grateful for my tennis and mock trial teams for enriching my life beyond the 9-5 with lessons I couldn't learn anywhere else. A big thank you to the New Jersey Scholars Program and my scholar family for playing intellectually with me. Together, we traverse the disciplines freely to learn just for fun, and that, to me, is priceless.

Thank you to my friends and weak ties who supported my book process and enjoyed the journey with me. Anna, our 2am punny loopy sessions not only exercise my wit and creativity but also fill my life with a laughter and childlike humor I cherish. Thank you to Rathi, Parker, Sahil, Frank, Chris, and Tiff, among others, for helping me get away with my crazy spontaneous last-minute pull-it-off moments and for making me smile along the way. Thank you to Eric, Brian, and New Degree Press for investing in my book and in me. Thank you also to all the people and stories I got to meet while writing this book— each of you has inspired me to commit to the unconventional.

My coaches and trainers, aka Jerry, you taught me grit. You taught me to be a competitive sportsman, put the team first, and hold the plank for 30 seconds more than I think I can. Thank you to all my sports for testing my physical and mental toughness.

Lastly, I am grateful for my health and peace of mind. Thank you to the universe for blessing me with a privileged life and an attitude of gratitude. I am thankful to all of you who spent time reading my words. I hope you learned something! More importantly, I hope you had fun.

APPENDIX

———

A BRIEF REFLECTION ON MY EDUCATION

Jason, Z. (2017). Bored Out of Their Minds. [online] Harvard Graduate School of Education. Available at: https://www.gse. harvard.edu/news/ed/17/01/bored-out-their-minds [Accessed 6 Nov. 2018].

INTRODUCTION

Christensen, Tanner, and Tanner Christensen. 2014. "Why Play Is Essential For Creativity". *Creative Something. Accessed November 7 2018. https://creativesomething.net/post/84134598535/ why-play-is-essential-for-creativity."Edward Lloyd And His Coffee House.". 2018. Lloyd's Register. Accessed November 7*

2018. https://www.lr.org/en/who-we-are/brief-history/edward-lloyd-coffee-house/.

"English Coffeehouses". 2018. *Historic UK. Accessed November 7 2018. https://www.historic-uk.com/CultureUK/English-Coffee-houses-Penny-Universities/.*

Green, Dr. 2017. "The Surprising History Of London's Fascinating (But Forgotten) Coffeehouses". *The Telegraph. Accessed November 6 2018.* https://www.telegraph.co.uk/travel/destinations/europe/united-kingdom/england/london/articles/London-cafes-the-surprising-history-of-Londons-lost-coffeehouses/.

"IBM 2010 Global CEO Study: Creativity Selected As Most Crucial Factor For Future Success". 2018. *Www-03.Ibm.Com. Accessed November 7 2018. https://www-03.ibm.com/press/us/en/press-release/31670.wss.*

Johnson, Steven. 2016. *Wonderland.*

Kelley, David. 2018. "How To Build Your Creative Confidence". *Ted. Com. Accessed November 7 2018. https://www.ted.com/talks/david_kelley_how_to_build_your_creative_confidence?language=en.*

"The Enlightenment Coffeehouses | Conversational Leadership". 2016. Conversational Leadership. Accessed November 7 2018. https://conversational-leadership.net/coffee-houses/.

CHAPTER 1
RECESS!

"American Time Use Survey: Charts By Topic: Leisure And Sports Activities". 2018. Bls.Gov. Accessed November 7 2018. https://www.bls.gov/tus/charts/leisure.htm.Devi, Gayatri. 2015. "Boredom Is Not A Problem To Be Solved. It's The Last Privilege Of A Free Mind | Gayatri Devi". The Guardian. Accessed November 7 2018. https://www.theguardian.com/commentisfree/2015/sep/28/boredom-cures-privilege-free-mind.Eastwood, John D., Alexandra Frischen, Mark J. Fenske, and Daniel Smilek. 2012. "The Unengaged Mind". Perspectives On Psychological Science 7 (5): 482–495. doi:10.1177/1745691612456044.

Gillett, Rachel. 2018. "13 Hobbies Highly Successful People Practice In Their Spare Time". Business Insider. Accessed November 7 2018. https://www.businessinsider.com/hobbies-highly-successful-people-do-in-their-spare-time-2016-7.

"Is Your Negativity Getting In The Way Of Your Creativity?". 2018. Big Think. Accessed November 7 2018. https://bigthink.com/good-news-you-can-overcome-negativity-bias.

Korda, Josh, About Korda, and Lion's Staff. 2017. "Boredom Is
Fascinating – – Josh Korda – Lion's Roar". Lion's Roar. Accessed
November 7 2018. https://www.lionsroar.com/this-is-how-you-
work-with-boredom/.

"Our Brain's Negative Bias". 2018. Psychology Today. Accessed
November 7 2018. https://www.psychologytoday.com/us/arti-
cles/200306/our-brains-negative-bias.

"Roger Federer's Mental Secret – Mindfulness-Based Tennis Psychology". 2018. Mindfulness-Based Tennis Psychology. Accessed
November 7 2018. https://www.tennismentalskills.com/rog-
er-federer-mental-game.

"TIP62: WARREN BUFFETT's FAVORITE BOOK, SECURITY
ANALYSIS". 2018. We Study Billionaires. Accessed November 7
2018. https://www.theinvestorspodcast.com/episodes/ep62-war-
ren-buffetts-favorite-book-security-analysis/.

"Young People Spend A Third Of Their Leisure Time On Devices
– Office For National Statistics". 2018. Ons.Gov.Uk. Accessed
November 7 2018. https://www.ons.gov.uk/peoplepopulation-
andcommunity/leisureandtourism/articles/youngpeoplespen-
dathirdoftheirleisuretimeondevices/2017–12–19.

Ward, Marguerite. 2016. "Warren Buffett's Reading Routine Could
Make You Smarter, Science Suggests". CNBC. Accessed Novem-

ber 7 2018. https://www.cnbc.com/2016/11/16/warren-buffetts-reading-routine-could-make-you-smarter-suggests-science.html.

CHAPTER 2
SLIDE

"Brain PNG – Pluspng". 2018. *Pluspng. Accessed November 9 2018. http://pluspng.com/brain-png-507.html.*

"Free Image On Pixabay – Stickman, Stick Figure". 2018. Pixabay. Com. Accessed November 9 2018. https://pixabay.com/en/stick-man-stick-figure-matchstick-man-151357/.

CHAPTER 3
PIRATES ON LAVA

05, Capítulo. 2015. "Capítulo 05". Donquijotedelamanchadecervantes.Blogspot.Com. Accessed November 22 2018. http://donquijotedelamanchadecervantes.blogspot.com/2015/03/capitulo-05.html.

Bellis, Mary. 2017. "Meet Arthur Fry: Inventor Of The Post-It Note". 2018. *Thoughtco. Accessed November 8 2018. https://www.thoughtco.com/history-of-post-it-note-1992326.Davis, Jeffrey. 2018. "The Science Of The Daydreaming Paradox For Innovation". Psychology Today.* https://www.psychologytoday.

com/us/blog/tracking-wonder/201708/the-science-the-day-dreaming-paradox-innovation.D'Onfro, Jillian. 2018. "The 'Absolute Worst Thing' Spacex Employees Can Say To Elon Musk ". *Business Insider. Accessed November 8 2018. https://www.businessinsider.com/elon-musk-doesnt-believe-in-impossible-2015–5.Ferro, Shaunacy. 2018. "How Imagination Works". Popsci.Com. https://www.popsci.com/science/article/2013–09/how-imagination-works.Hertzfeld, Andy, Steve Capps, Donn Denman, Bruce Horn, and Susan Kare. n.d. Revolution In The Valley.*

"El Ingenioso Hidalgo De Don Quijote De La Mancha. Capítulo IV". 2018. Elmundo.Es. Accessed November 22 2018. https://www.elmundo.es/quijote/capitulo.html?cual=4.

"Historical Context For Don Quixote By Miguel De Cervantes | The Core Curriculum". 2018. *College.Columbia.Edu. Accessed November 8 2018. https://www.college.columbia.edu/core/node/1764.*

"How Steve Jobs Created The Reality Distortion Field (And You Can, Too)". 2016. Medium. Accessed November 8 2018. https://medium.com/@jhargrave/how-steve-jobs-created-the-reality-distortion-field-and-you-can-too-4ba87781adba.

Johnson, Craig E, and Michael Z Hackman. 2013. *Leadership.Lehrer, Jonah. 2012. Imagine. [Grand Haven, Ml]: Brilliance Audio.*

Mooneyham, Benjamin W., and Jonathan W. Schooler. 2013. "The Costs And Benefits Of Mind-Wandering: A Review.". Canadian Journal Of Experimental Psychology/Revue Canadienne De Psychologie Expérimentale 67 (1): 11–18. doi:10.1037/a0031569. Pillay, Srinivasan S. n.d. Tinker Dabble Doodle Try.

"What Is A Reality Distortion Field? – Definition From Techopedia". 2018. Techopedia.Com. Accessed November 9 2018. https://www.techopedia.com/definition/23694/reality-distortion-field-rdf.

CHAPTER 4
DIGGING FOR WORMS

Ahmed, Muneer. 2011. "Openideo – 7 Tips On Better Brainstorming". Challenges.Openideo.Com. Accessed November 8 2018. https://challenges.openideo.com/blog/seven-tips-on-better-brainstorming.

"Design Thinking: A Method For Creative Problem Solving". 2018. IDEO U. Accessed November 8 2018. https://www.ideou.com/pages/design-thinking.

"Divergent Thinking And The Innovation Funnel". 2018. IDEO U. Accessed November 8 2018. https://www.ideou.com/blogs/inspiration/brendan-boyle-on-divergent-thinking-and-the-innovation-funnel.Dubner, Stephen J, and Steven D Levitt. 2015. Think Like A Freak. HarperCollins USA.Easley, David, and Jon

Kleinberg. 2018. *Networks, Crowds, And Markets. Johanneshov: MTM.Editors, History.com. 2018. "Jenner Tests Smallpox Vaccine". HISTORY. Accessed November 8 2018.* https://www.history.com/this-day-in-history/jenner-tests-smallpox-vaccine.

Riedel, Stefan. 2005. "Edward Jenner And The History Of Smallpox And Vaccination". *Proceedings (Baylor University. Medical Center) 18 (1): 21. https://www.ncbi.nlm.nih.gov/pmc/articles/PMC1200696/.*

Routson, Joyce. 2011. *"Embracing A Way To Change The World". 2018. Stanford Graduate School Of Business. Accessed November 8 2018. https://www.gsb.stanford.edu/insights/embracing-way-change-world.*

Kelley, David. 2018. *"How To Build Your Creative Confidence". Ted. Com. Accessed November 8 2018.* https://www.ted.com/talks/david_kelley_how_to_build_your_creative_confidence?language=en.

Kelley, Tom, and David Kelley. 2012 "Reclaim Your Creative Confidence". 2012. *Harvard Business Review. Accessed November 8 2018. https://hbr.org/2012/12/reclaim-your-creative-confidence.*

Kelley, Tom, and David Kelley. 2013 "Slate's Use Of Your Data". 2018. *Slate Magazine. Accessed November 8 2018. https://slate.com/human-interest/2013/10/creative-confidence-a-new-book-from-*

ideo-s-tom-and-david-kelley.html.Kelley, Tom, and David Kelley. 2015. Creative Confidence. London: William Collins.

"Open Source | IDEO Labs | Page 4". 2018. *Labs.Ideo.Com. Accessed November 8 2018.* https://labs.ideo.com/category/open-source/page/4/.

"The Business Value Of Design". 2018. *Mckinsey & Company. Accessed November 8 2018. https://www.mckinsey.com/business-functions/mckinsey-design/our-insights/the-business-value-of-design.*

Schwab, Katharine. 2018. "This Mckinsey Study Of 300 Companies Reveals What Every Business Needs To Know About Design For 2019". 2018. *Fast Company. Accessed November 8 2018. https://www.fastcompany.com/90255363/this-mckinsey-study-of-300-companies-reveals-what-every-business-needs-to-know-about-design-for-2019?partner=rss&utm_source=facebook.com&utm_medium=social&utm_campaign=rss+fastcompany&utm_content=rss.*

"The Scientific Method". 2018. *Khan Academy. Accessed November 8 2018. https://www.khanacademy.org/science/high-school-biology/hs-biology-foundations/hs-biology-and-the-scientific-method/a/the-science-of-biology.*

"What Is Design Thinking?". 2018. *IDEO U. Accessed November 8 2018.* https://www.ideou.com/blogs/inspiration/what-is-design-thinking.White, Ed, and Ed White. 2018. "Down On The (Digital) Farm | IDEO Labs". *Labs.Ideo.Com. Accessed November 8 2018.* https://labs.ideo.com/2016/06/08/down-on-the-digital-farm/.

CHAPTER 5
MONKEY BARS

Bandura, Albert. 1977. "Self-Efficacy: Toward A Unifying Theory Of Behavioral Change.". *Psychological Review 84 (2): 191–215. doi:10.1037//0033–295x.84.2.191.Bariso, Justin. 2018. "12 Brilliant Quotes From The Genius Mind Of Sir Isaac Newton". 2016. Inc. Com. Accessed November 8 2018. https://www.inc.com/justin-bariso/12-brilliant-quotes-from-the-genius-mind-of-sir-isaac-newton.html.Dubner, Stephen J, and Steven D Levitt. 2015. Think Like A Freak. HarperCollins USA.*

Kelley, Tom, and David Kelley. 2012 "Reclaim Your Creative Confidence". 2012. *Harvard Business Review. Accessed November 8 2018. https://hbr.org/2012/12/reclaim-your-creative-confidence.*

Grant, Heidi. 2013. *"Do You Play To Win—Or To Not Lose?". 2013. Harvard Business Review. Accessed November 8 2018.* https://hbr.org/2013/03/do-you-play-to-win-or-to-not-lose.

Phung, Albert. "Behavioral Finance: Key Concepts – Prospect Theory". 2007. *Investopedia. Accessed November 8 2018.* https://
www.investopedia.com/university/behavioral_finance/behav-
ioral11.asp.Robinson, Ken, and Lou Aronica. 2014. *The Element. New York: Penguin Books.Whipps, Heather. Science, Live.
2008. "How Isaac Newton Changed The World". Live Science.
Accessed November 8 2018.* https://www.livescience.com/4965-
isaac-newton-changed-world.html.Yang, Andrew. 2014. *Smart
People Should Build Things.*

CHAPTER 6
TAG

Clear, James. 2013. "How To Deal With Judgment And Criticism In
A Healthy Way". 2013. *Lifehacker Australia. Accessed November
8 2018.* https://www.lifehacker.com.au/2013/10/how-to-deal-
with-judgment-and-criticism-in-a-healthy-way/.Easley, David,
and Jon Kleinberg. 2018. *Networks, Crowds, And Markets.
Johanneshov: MTM.Jenkins, Aric. "Survey Finds That Half of
Americans – Especially Young People – Feel Lonely". 2018. Fortune. Accessed November 8 2018.* http://fortune.com/2018/05/01/
americans-lonely-cigna-study/.

" Maria Montessori Biography And History | American Montessori
Society ". 2018. *Amshq.Org. Accessed November 8 2018.* https://
amshq.org/Montessori-Education/History-of-Montessori-Ed-
ucation/Biography-of-Maria-Montessori.

"Pete Carroll In 60 Minutes". 2008. *Vimeo. Accessed November 8 2018. https://vimeo.com/2529346.*"The First Casa Dei Bambini | Montessori Australia Foundation". 2018. Montessori.Org.Au. Accessed November 8 2018. https://montessori.org.au/first-casa-dei-bambini.*

Trotter, Jim. 2014. "The power of positive coaching." Accessed November 8 2018. https://www.si.com/2014/01/23/pete-carroll-seattle-seahawks-super-bowl-48.

Ramakrishnan, Dinesh. 2018. "What Are The Drawbacks Of Bohr's Theory?". *Infofavour.Blogspot.Com. Accessed November 8 2018. https://infofavour.blogspot.com/2014/06/what-are-drawbacks-of-bohrs-theory.html.*

CHAPTER 7
COLOR OUTSIDE

Bell, Chris. 2013. "Monsters University: What's It Like To Work At Pixar? ". *Telegraph.Co.Uk. Accessed November 8 2018. https://www.telegraph.co.uk/culture/film/10144531/Monsters-University-whats-it-like-to-work-at-Pixar.html.*

Catmull, Ed. 2008. *"How Pixar Fosters Collective Creativity". 2008. Harvard Business Review. Accessed November 8 2018.* https://hbr.org/2008/09/how-pixar-fosters-collective-creativity.

Dyer, Jennifer. "The Innovator'S DNA". 2009. *Harvard Business Review. Accessed November 8 2018. https://hbr.org/2009/12/ the-innovators-dna.*

Feinberg, Danielle. 2018. "The Magic Ingredient That Brings Pixar Movies To Life". *Ted.Com. Accessed November 8 2018.* https://www.ted.com/talks/danielle_feinberg_the_magic_ingredient_that_brings_pixar_movies_to_life?language=en.

Johansson, Frans. 2006. *The Medici Effect. Boston, Mass.: Harvard Business School Press.Newport, Cal. 2016. Deep Work.*

Scientists, Top, and List Scientists. 2018. "Adolphe Quetelet". *Famousscientists.Org. Accessed November 8 2018. https://www. famousscientists.org/adolphe-quetelet/.*

CHAPTER 8
ON THE FIELD

2018. *Creativityworkshop.Com. Accessed November 8 2018. https:// creativityworkshop.com/articles/travelandcreativity.*

Clarey, Christopher. 2017. "Roger Federer, Defying Age, Tops Rafael Nadal In Australian Open Final". *Nytimes.Com. Accessed November 8 2018.* https://www.nytimes.com/2017/01/29/sports/ tennis/roger-federer-rafael-nadal-australian-open.html.

Crane, Brent. 2015. "For A More Creative Brain, Travel". *The Atlantic. Accessed November 8 2018. https://www.theatlantic.com/health/archive/2015/03/for-a-more-creative-brain-travel/388135/.*

Fondas, Nanette. "Research: More Than Half Of Top Female Execs Were College Athletes". 2014. Harvard Business Review. Accessed November 8 2018. https://hbr.org/2014/10/research-more-than-half-of-female-execs-were-college-athletes.

Hall, Mark. 2018. "From Athlete To Entrepreneur: An Interview About Why The Tech Industry Attracts So Many Sports Stars". Forbes. Accessed November 8 2018. https://www.forbes.com/sites/markhall/2018/04/17/from-athlete-to-entrepreneur/#55bb3d2456c8.

High, Peter. 2018. "The Secret Ingredient Of Successful People And Organizations: Grit". Forbes. Accessed November 8 2018. https://www.forbes.com/sites/peterhigh/2016/05/23/the-secret-ingredient-of-successful-people-and-organizations-grit/#24ef19a262ef.

Lebowitz, Shana. 2018. "A Single High School In India Has Produced The Ceos Of Microsoft, Adobe, And Mastercard". Business Insider. Accessed November 8 2018. https://www.businessinsider.com/microsoft-adobe-mastercard-ceos-went-to-same-high-school-2018–3?utm_content=buffer-5366d&utm_medium=social&utm_source=facebook.com&utm_campaign=buffer-ti&fbclid=IwAR1vWbgWL-

cP9c1cchvQ8giF_R9gzwoY35yzuw3VHhQ4PePdsS2qlCDX-Djb8.Mcaffrey, Vin. *"GTG Featured In EY Women Athletes & ESPNW Study – Game Plan".* 2015. *Game Plan. Accessed November 8 2018.* http://wearegameplan.com/blog/gtg-featured-in-ey-women-athletes-espnw-study/.

Menayang, Adi. 2017. "The Brothers Behind Sunniva Super Coffee Tap Into Student Demand For More Energy". 2017. *Foodnavigator-Usa.Com. Accessed November 8 2018. https://www. foodnavigator-usa.com/Article/2017/04/04/Sunniva-Super-Coffee-taps-into-student-demand-for-more-energy#.*

Rohan, Lysha. *"How Travel Makes You More Creative | Travel Helps Creativity".* 2017. *Nomads – Discover Different. Accessed November 8 2018.* https://nomadsworld.com/travel-helps-creativity/.

Sagal, Peter. 2018. "The Case Against Running With Headphones". *Nytimes.Com. Accessed November 8 2018. https://www.nytimes. com/2018/10/30/well/move/peter-sagal-book-running-without-headphones.html.*

Sugar, Rachel. 2018. *"Researchers Have A Theory To Explain Why High-School Athletes Go On To Be Successful In Life". Business Insider. Accessed November 8 2018. https://www.businessinsider. com/why-athletes-make-good-employees-2015-6.*

"The Sublime". 2018. Webpages.Uidaho.Edu. Accessed November 8 2018. https://www.webpages.uidaho.edu/engl_258/Lecture%20 Notes/sublime.htm.

University, Stanford. "Stanford Study Finds Walking Improves Creativity". Stanford News. Accessed November 8 2018. https://news.stanford.edu/2014/04/24/walking-vs-sitting-042414/.

"Women 2000 and Beyond."2018. Un.Org. Accessed November 8 2018. http://www.un.org/womenwatch/daw/public/Women%20 and%20Sport.pdf.

CHAPTER 9
SANDCASTLES

"4 Unexpected Ways A Startup Can Accelerate Your Career". 2015. Themuse.Com. Accessed November 8 2018. https://www.themuse.com/advice/4-unexpected-ways-a-startup-can-accelerate-your-career.

Adams, Susan. 2018. "Unhappy Employees Outnumber Happy Ones By Two To One Worldwide". Forbes. Accessed November 8 2018. https://www.forbes.com/sites/susanadams/2013/10/10/unhappy-employees-outnumber-happy-ones-by-two-to-one-worldwide/#630bf73c362a.

"Alberobello Tourist Information | Italy Heaven". 2018. Italyheaven. Co.Uk. Accessed November 8 2018. http://www.italyheaven. co.uk/puglia/alberobello.html.

Carther, Shauna. 2003. "Understanding The Time Value Of Money". Investopedia. Accessed November 8 2018. https://www.investo-pedia.com/articles/03/082703.asp.

"College: Capital Or Signal? | Economic Man". 2018. Economic-manblog.Com. Accessed November 8 2018. http://www.eco-nomicmanblog.com/college-capital-or-signal/.Gallup, Inc. 2017. "Do You Regret Your College Choices?". Gallup.Com. Accessed November 8 2018. https://news.gallup.com/opinion/ gallup/211070/regret-college-choices.aspx.

"Genetic Variation And Natural Selection: Natural Selection". 2018. Infoplease. Accessed November 8 2018. https://www.infoplease. com/science/biology/genetic-variation-and-natural-selec-tion-natural-selection.

Glancey, Jonathan. 2001. "The Folly Of Fallingwater". The Guard-ian. Accessed November 8 2018. https://www.theguardian.com/ culture/2001/sep/10/artsfeatures.

Gustafson, Bob. 2015. "Portfolio Rebalancing – Balancing Risk And Return". Triton Financial Group. Accessed November 8 2018. https://tritonfinancialgroup.com/portfolio-rebalancing/.

Kiener, Maximilian. 2018. "Why Time Flies". *Maximiliankiener. Com. Accessed November 8 2018. https://www.maximiliankiener.com/digitalprojects/time/.*

Kiyosaki, Robert T, John Fleming, and Kim Kiyosaki. 2013. *The Business Of The 21St Century. Lake Dallas, Tex.: Success Partners.Stillman, Jessica. 2018. "Elon Musk To The Young And Ambitious: Skills Matter More Than Degrees". 2017. Inc.Com. Accessed November 8 2018.* https://www.inc.com/jessica-stillman/why-elon-musk-doesnt-care-about-college-degrees.html. Simmons, Michael. 2017. "5-Hour Rule: If You'Re Not Spending 5 Hours Per Week Learning, You'Re Being Irresponsible". 2017. *Medium. Accessed November 8 2018. https://medium.com/the-mission/the-5-hour-rule-if-youre-not-spending-5-hours-per-week-learning-you-re-being-irresponsible-791c3f18f5e6.*

SCHOOL'S OUT

Robinson, Ken. 2018. "Do Schools Kill Creativity?". Ted.Com. Accessed November 21 2018. https://www.ted.com/talks/ken_robinson_says_schools_kill_creativity?language=en.

"What Schools Can Learn From Google, IDEO, And Pixar". 2011. Fast Company. Accessed November 21 2018. https://www.fastcompany. com/1664735/what-schools-can-learn-from-google-ideo-and-pixar.

Made in the USA
Monee, IL
29 April 2021

67261824R00164